Molly Davies

God Bless the Child

Bloomsbury Methuen Drama
An imprint of Bloomsbury Publishing Plc

B L O O M S B U R Y
LONDON • NEW DELHI • NEW YORK • SYDNEY

Bloomsbury Methuen Drama

An imprint of Bloomsbury Publishing Plc

Imprint previously known as Methuen Drama

50 Bedford Square	1385 Broadway
London	New York
WC1B 3DP	NY 10018
UK	USA

www.bloomsbury.com

BLOOMSBURY, METHUEN DRAMA and the Diana logo
are trademarks of Bloomsbury Publishing Plc

First published 2015

© Molly Davies 2015

British Library Cataloguing-in-Publication Data
A catalogue record for this book is available from the British Library

ISBN: PB: 978-1-4742-2188-7
ePDF: 978-1-4742-2189-4
ePub: 978-1-4742-2190-0

Library of Congress Cataloging-in-Publication Data
A catalog record for this book is available from the Library of Congress

Typeset by Country Setting, Kingsdown, Kent CT14 8ES
Printed and bound in Great Britain

THE ROYAL COURT
THEATRE PRESENTS

GOD BLESS THE CHILD

By Molly Davies

God Bless the Child was first performed at the Royal Court Jerwood Theatre Upstairs, Sloane Square, on Wednesday 12th November 2014.

God Bless the Child is part of the Royal Court's Jerwood New Playwrights Programme, supported by the Jerwood Charitable Foundation.

GOD BLESS THE CHILD
BY MOLLY DAVIES

CAST

CLASS OF 4N

Orange Team
Esther **Lizzie Wells**
Freddie **Cedric Essumang**
Grace **Grace Taylor**
Jake **Colby Mulgrew**
Lily **Beatrice Playfoot-Orme**
Louis **Bobby Smalldridge**
Tamaya **Lahaina Asumang**

Green Team
Aaron **Darwin Brokenbro**
Esther **Maleah Rutty**
Freddie **Joseph West**
Grace **Lara Decaro**
Jake **David Evans**
Lily **Tyla Wilson**
Louie **Nancy Allsop**
Tamaya **Zahra O'Reilly**

ADULT CAST

Sali Rayner **Amanda Abbington**
Ms Evitt **Nikki Amuka Bird**
Mrs Bradley **Julie Hesmondhalgh**
Ms Newsome **Ony Uhiara**

GOD BLESS THE CHILD
BY MOLLY DAVIES

Director **Vicky Featherstone**
Designer **Chloe Lamford**
Lighting Designer **Philip Gladwell**
Composer & Sound Designer **Mark Melville**
Movement Director **Imogen Knight**
Associate Designer **Ruth Stringer**
Assistant Director **Debbie Hannan**
Casting Director **Amy Ball**
Production Manager **Tariq Rifaat**
Stage Managers **Sophie Rubenstein/Sarah Hopkins**
Stage Management Work Placement **Kate Ashford**
Costume Supervisor **Holly White**
Chaperones **Elaine Henderson-Boyle/Justin Kielty**
Set built by **Royal Court Theatre Stage Department**
Ceiling Installed by **Ceilings & Interiors (UK) Ltd.**
Set Painted by **Zoe Hurwitz**

The Royal Court and Stage Management wish to thank the following for their help with this production:
**Josie Bending, George Eliot Primary School, Holy Trinity Church of England
Primary School, Pikemere Primary School, Katie Rubenstein at Longfield Primary
School, Melisha Trotman at Crowley Primary School, Young Vic.**

GOD BLESS THE CHILD
THE COMPANY

Molly Davies (Writer)

For the Royal Court: **A Miracle.**

Other theatre includes: **Orpheus & Eurydice** (NYT/Old Vic Tunnels); **Shooting Truth** (National); **The Future of Bump** (Hampstead); **My Days** (Soho/Company of Angels); **Fragile** (Shared Experience); **The Birds Stopped Singing** (Company of Angels).

Amanda Abbington (Sali Rayner)

Theatre includes: **Love Me Tonight** (Hampstead); **The Safari Party** (Stephen Joseph, Scarborough/Hampstead); **Something Blue** (Stephen Joseph, Scarborough); **Tin Soldiers** (New End/Grace).

Television includes: **Mr Selfridge, Dinopaws, Sherlock, Case Histories, Joe Mistry, Open Doors, Being Human, Post Code, Money, Married. Single. Other., Psychoville, Harley Street, Poirot, Doc Martin, The Bill, Man Stroke Woman, After You've Gone, Booze Cruise, Derailed, The Robinsons, Teachers, Coupling, Bernhard's Watch, 20 Things To Do Before You're 30, The Debt, Always & Everyone, Hearts & Bones, Men Only, Shades, Sins, Dream Team, The Thing About Vince, Snap, Plotlands, No Sweat, Casualty.**

Film includes: **Ghosted, Swinging With the Finkels, The All Together, The Good Night.**

Radio includes: **Life in London, Clement Doesn't Live Here Anymore.**

Nancy Allsop (Louie)

Theatre includes: **Annie** (Waterside, Aylesbury); **Whistle Down the Wind, The Sound of Music** (Court, Pendley Tring).

Nikki Amuka-Bird (Ms Evitt)

For the Royal Court: **Birdland, Love & Information.**

Theatre includes: **The Trial of Ubu** (Hampstead); **Welcome to Thebes** (National); **Doubt** (Tricycle); **Twelfth Night** (Bristol Old Vic); **World Music** (Donmar); **A Midsummer Night's Dream, The Tempest, The Servant of Two Masters** (RSC); **Top Girls, 50 Revolutions** (Oxford Stage Company).

Television includes: **Scrotal Recall, Quarry, Luther, House of Fools Survivors, Small Island, The No. 1 Ladies' Detective Agency, Torchwood, The Last Enemy, Whistleblower, Five Days, Born Equal, Shoot the Messenger, Robin Hood, Spooks, Crime Monologues: Grace, The Line of Beauty, Afterlife, Murder Prevention, The Canterbury Tales: Man of Law's Tale, NCS Manhunt, Always Be Closing, Grafters.**

Film includes: **The Face of an Angel, Jupiter Ascending, Coriolanus, The Disappeared, The Omen, Cargo, Almost Heaven.**

Radio includes: **When the Laughter Stops, Words & Music, Noughts & Crosses, Charity, Man In Black, The Lucky Girl, White Shoes, Charity, England, The Colour Purple, Mister Pip, Free Juice for All, The No. 1 Ladies' Detective Agency, Top Girls, Lady Play, Troilus & Cressida.**

Lahaina Asumung (Tamaya)

This is Lahaina's professional stage debut.

Television includes: **Midsomer Murders.**

Opera includes: **The Magic Flute** (ENO).

Darwin Brokenbro (Aaron)

This is Darwin's professional stage debut.

Television includes: **The Tunnel, Fortitude.**

Lara Decaro (Grace)

Theatre includes: **Les Misérables, The Wizard of Oz** (West End).

Television includes: **Fortitude.**

Film includes: **Criminal.**

Cedric Essumang (Freddie)

This is Cedric's professional stage debut.

Television Includes: **EastEnders**

David Evans (Jake)

This is David's professional stage debut.

Television includes: **Silent Witness, Peep Show.**

Vicky Featherstone (Director)

For the Royal Court: **Maidan: Voices from the Uprising, The Mistress Contract, The Ritual Slaughter of Gorge Mastromas, Untitled Matriarch Play, The President Has Come to See You (Open Court Weekly Rep).**

Other theatre includes: **Enquirer (co-director), An Appointment with the Wicker Man, 27, The Wheel, Somersaults, Wall of Death: A Way of Life (co-director), The Miracle Man, Empty, Long Gone Lonesome (National Theatre of Scotland); Cockroach (National Theatre of Scotland/Traverse); 365 (National Theatre of Scotland/Edinburgh International Festival); Mary Stuart (National Theatre of Scotland/Citizens/Royal Lyceum, Edinburgh); The Wolves in the Walls (co-director) (National Theatre of Scotland/Improbable/Tramway/Lyric, Hammersmith/UK tour/New Victory, New York); The Small Things, Pyrenees, The Drowned World, Tiny Dynamite, Crazy Gary's Mobile Disco, Splendour, Riddance, The Cosmonaut's Last Message to the Woman He Once Loved in the Former Soviet Union, Crave (Paines Plough).**

Created for television: **Where the Heart Is, Silent Witness.**

Vicky was Artistic Director of Paines Plough 1997-2005 and the founding Artistic Director of The National Theatre of Scotland 2005-2012.

Vicky is the Artistic Director of the Royal Court.

Philip Gladwell (Lighting Designer)

For the Royal Court: **The Ritual Slaughter of Gorge Mastromas, No Quarter, Oxford Street, Kebab.**
Other theatre includes: **The James Plays, The World of Extreme Happiness, Love the Sinner (National); The Infidel (Theatre Royal Stratford East); Mr Burns, Before the Party (Almeida); Hairspray, Chicago, Obama the Mamba, Gypsy (Curve, Leicester); Happy Days, The King & I, Radio Times (UK tour); Ciara, I'm With the Band, The Arthur Conan Doyle Appreciation Society (Traverse); LIMBO (London Wonderground & International tour); Miss Julie (Barbican/Schaubühne, Berlin); A Midsummer Night's Dream (Barbican/Bristol Old Vic/Spoleto Festival, USA); Enjoy (West Yorkshire Playhouse); Pastoral (Soho); The Opinion Makers (Mercury, Colchester/Derby); Every Last Trick, One For The Road, The Duchess of Malfi, Blood Wedding (Royal & Derngate); If Only (Chichester Festival); Further Than the Furthest Thing (Dundee Rep); Amazonia, Ghosts, The Member of the Wedding, Festa! (Young Vic); Cinderella, Aladdin, Mogadishu, Punk Rock (Lyric Hammersmith); Too Clever By Half, You Can't Take It With You, Nineteen Eighty-Four, Macbeth (Royal Exchange, Manchester); The Fahrenheit Twins, Low Pay? Don't Pay! (Told by an Idiot).**

Debbie Hannan (Assistant Director)

As Director, for the Royal Court: **Spaghetti Ocean, Peckham: The Soap Opera (co-director).**

As Assistant Director, for the Royal Court: **Teh Internet is Serious Business, The Nether, Primetime, Birdland, The Mistress Contract.**

As Director, other theatre includes: **Notes from the Underground (Citizens); Panorama, Roses Are Dead, You Cannot Call it Love (Arches); Yellow Pears (Swept Up); liberty, equality, fraternity (Tron/Traverse).**

As Associate Director, other theatre includes: **Little on the Inside (Clean Break).**

As Assistant Director, other theatre includes: **A Doll's House, Enquirer (National Theatre of Scotland/Royal Lyceum, Edinburgh); The Maids, Beauty & the Beast (Citizens); Kurt Weill: Double Bill (Scottish Opera); War of the Roses Trilogy (Bard in the Botanics); Hamlet (Globe Education).**

Debbie is Trainee Director at the Royal Court.

Julie Hesmondhalgh
(Mrs Bradley)

Theatre includes: **Blindsided, Black Roses: The Killing of Sophie Lancaster, Much Ado About Nothing (Royal Exchange,**

Manchester); The Play What I Wrote (David Pugh Ltd); Waking Beauty, The Secret of the White Rose, Bar & Ger, Statements After An Arrest Under The Immorality Act, The Tempest, A Dance With My Memories, The Lizzie Play (Arts Threshold); The Lizzie Play (Jackson's Lane/Theatre Clwyd Studio/National tour).

Television includes: **Cucumber, Banana, Coronation Street, Black Roses, Dalziel & Pascoe, The Bill, Pat & Margaret, Catherine Cookson's The Dwelling Place.**

Imogen Knight
(Movement Director)

As Choreographer, for the Royal Court: **Love, Love, Love.**

As Movement Director, for the Royal Court: **The Low Road, A Time to Reap.**

Other Theatre Includes: **Hamlet, Blindsided, Cannibals** (Royal Exchange, Manchester); **Dirty Butterfly** (Young Vic); **'Tis Pity She's A Whore** (Globe); **Little Revolution, Measure for Measure** (Almeida); **The Crucible** (Old Vic); **Red Velvet** (Tricycle/St Anne's Warehouse, New York); **Edward II** (National); **In Time O'Strife, An Appointment with the Wicker Man, The Missing** (National Theatre of Scotland); **The History Boys** (Sheffield Crucible); **but i cd only whisper** (Arcola); **One Day When We Were Young, The Sound of Heavy Rain** (Paines Plough); **As You Like It** (West Yorkshire Playhouse); **Corrie** (Lowry/UK tour).

Dance Includes: **Under the Carpet** (De Stilte, Holland); **OMG!** (Sadler's Wells/ Company of Angels/The Place); **Penelope** (Dramaturgs Network/ Company of Angels).

Opera Includes: **Powder Her Face** (ENO); **How To Make An Opera, The Little Sweep** (Malmo).

Television includes: **The Hollow Crown, Call the Midwife.**

Imogen was previously an Associate Artist with Frantic Assembly. She is also a guest lecturer in Movement at Central School of Speech and Drama.

Chloe Lamford (Designer)

For the Royal Court: **2071, Teh Internet is Serious Business, Open Court, Circle Mirror Transformation.**
Other theatre includes: **Salt Root & Roe**

(Donmar/Trafalgar Studios); **Praxis Makes Perfect** (National Theatre Wales); **Lungs** (Schaubühne, Berlin); **1984** (Headlong/Almeida/West End/ tour); **The World of Extreme Happiness** (National); **Boys** (Headlong); **Cannibals, The Gate Keeper** (Royal Exchange, Manchester); **The Events** (Actors Touring Company/Young Vic/tour); **The History Boys** (Crucible, Sheffield); **Disco Pigs, Sus, Blackta** (Young Vic); **My Shrinking Life, An Appointment With the Wicker Man, Knives in Hens** (National Theatre of Scotland); **The Radicalisation of Bradley Manning** (National Theatre Wales/Edinburgh International Festival); **Ghost Story** (Sky Arts Live Drama); **Britannicus** (Wilton's Music Hall); **My Romantic History** (Crucible, Sheffield/Bush); **Joseph K, The Kreutzer Sonata** (Gate); **Songs From A Hotel Bedroom** (Royal Opera House/tour); **it felt empty when the heart went at first but it is alright now, This Wide Night** (Clean Break); **The Mother Ship, How to Tell the Monsters from the Misfits** (Birmingham Rep); **Small Miracle** (Tricycle/Mercury, Colchester).

Awards Include: **Theatrical Management Association Award for Best Theatre Design** (Small Miracle); **Arts Foundation Fellowship Award for Design for Performance: Set & Costume.**

Mark Melville
(Composer & Sound Designer)

Theatre Includes: **Hamlet, Your Country Needs You (but I don't need my country), No Fat Juliets, Robin Hood, Pierrepoint, The Unsociables, The BFG, Two, Merlin, Quicksand, The Snow Queen, Peter Pan, Children of Killers, Of Mice & Men, Jason & The Argonauts** (Duke's Playhouse); **Tomorrow** (Vanishing Point/Cena Contemporânea Festival, Brasil/Brighton Festival/ Tramway/National); **Dragon** (Vox Motus/National Theatre of Scotland/ Tianjin People's Art Theatre, China); **The Beautiful Cosmos of Ivor Cutler** (Vanishing Point/National Theatre of Scotland); **Swallows & Amazons, Grimm Tales** (Theatre by the Lake); **Saturday Night** (Vanishing Point/National Theatre of Portugal); **Knives in Hens, Miracle Man, Empty, My Shrinking Life** (National Theatre of Scotland); **Pride & Prejudice** (Two Bit Classics); **Mister Holgado** (Unicorn); **A Midsummer**

Night's Dream (Royal Lyceum, Edinburgh); Wonderland (Vanishing Point/Napoli Teatro Festival Italia/Tramway/Edinburgh International Festival); Mwana (Ankur/Tron); The Beggars Opera (Vanishing Point/Royal Lyceum, Edinburgh/Belgrade, Coventry); What Happened Was This, One Night Stand, Naked Neighbour Twitching Blind (Never Did Nothing/Tron/Tramway).

Dance Includes: **In a Deep Dark Wood (Gobbledegook/Moko Dance); Best Friends (M6/Ludus);**

Awards Include: **Critics Award for Theatre in Scotland for Best Technical Presentation (Dragon); Critics Award for Theatre for Best Music & Sound (The Beautiful Cosmos of Ivor Cutler); UK Theatre Award for Best Show for Children & Young People (Mister Holgado).**

Mark is an Associate Artist of The Duke's Playhouse.

Colby Mulgrew (Jake)

Theatre includes: **Billy Elliot, Scrooge, Matilda (West End).**

Zahra O'Reilly (Tamaya)

This is Zahra's professional stage debut.

Beatrice Playfoot-Orme (Lily)

For the Royal Court: **Adler & Gibb.**

Film includes: **Albert, Plugged In, Soror.**

Maleah Rutty (Esther)

This is Maleah's professional stage debut.

Bobby Smalldridge (Louis)

Theatre includes: **Billy Elliot (West End)**

Television includes: **Agatha Christie's Marple: Greenshaw's Folly, Casualty, Cockroaches.**

Film includes: **Foster, What We Did on Our Holiday.**

Ruth Stringer (Associate Designer)

As Assistant Designer, for the Royal Court: **Open Court.**

As Designer, other theatre includes: **Green Man, Red Woman (National Theatre Wales/Green Man Festival); Soho Young Playwrights (Soho); Rush (Alma Tavern);**

Forest: The Nature of Crisis (Constanza Macras/Dorky Park/Schaubühne, Berlin), Branches: The Nature of Crisis (National Theatre Wales/Constanza Macras/Dorky Park).**

As Assistant Designer, other theatre includes: **Praxis Makes Perfect (National Theatre Wales/Neon Neon); Coriolan/us (National Theatre Wales/RSC); The Passion (National Theatre Wales/Wildworks).**

Grace Taylor (Grace)

This is Grace's professional stage debut.

Ony Uhiara (Ms Newsome)

For the Royal Court: **Motor Town, Fallout.**

Other theatre includes: **Eye of a Needle (Southwark Playhouse); Idomeneus, How To Be An Other Woman (Gate); The El Train (Hoxton Hall); Cannibals (Royal Exchange, Manchester); Illusions (Actors Touring Company); Sixty-Six Books (Bush); Much Ado About Nothing (Globe); Charged: Dancing Bears (Soho); Eurydice (Young Vic/tour); In the Red & Brown Water (Young Vic); Noughts & Crosses, Pericles, The Winter's Tale, Days of Significance (RSC); Silverland (Lacuna); Walk Hard, Talk Loud (Tricycle); The Seer, Medea (West Yorkshire Playhouse).**

Television includes: **Law & Order, Stolen, White Van Man, Criminal Justice, Barclay, Doctors, Rosemary & Thyme, The Bill, Proof, Holby City, Snowman, M.I.T., The Crouches, Waking the Dead, The Vice.**

Film includes: **Venus, Sixty 6.**

Lizzie Wells (Esther)

This is Lizzie's professional stage debut.

Joseph West (Freddie)

Theatre includes: **Merrily We Roll Along, Billy Elliot (West End).**

Television includes: **Roald Dahl's Esio Trot, It's Kevin, Ministry of Curious Stuff.**

Film includes: **Les Miserables, Nativity!, Nativity 2: Danger in the Manger!.**

Tyla Wilson (Lily)

Theatre includes: **Cinderella (Swan, High Wycombe).**

NEW SEASON
UNTIL MAY 2015

"All of these plays are about revolutions – big and small acts of resistance. They are provocative, diverse and timely. They are great stories, inventively told and demanding that we consider a better future"

Vicky Featherstone
Artistic Director

JERWOOD THEATRE
UPSTAIRS

7 – 31 Jan
Liberian Girl
By Diana
Nneka Atuona

This Alfred Fagon award-winning play tells one teenage girl's story of survival.

12 Feb – 14 Mar
Fireworks
by Dalia Taha

This new Palestinian play gives us a new way of seeing how war fractures childhood.

JERWOOD THEATRE
DOWNSTAIRS

5 – 15 Nov
2071
By Duncan Macmillan and Chris Rapley

A new piece of theatre has been created, with Director Katie Mitchell, where science is centre stage.

A co-operation with Deutsches Schauspielhaus, Hamburg

26 Nov – 10 Jan
Hope
By Jack Thorne

A funny and scathing fable attacking the squeeze on local government.

4 Feb – 21 Mar
How To Hold Your Breath
By Zinnie Harris

An epic look at the true cost of principles and how we live now.

7 Apr – 31 May
Roald Dahl's
The Twits
By Enda Walsh

Mischievously adapted from one of the world's most loved books, Enda Walsh turns the The Twits upside down.

020 7565 5000 (no booking fee)
royalcourttheatre.com

Follow us 🐦 royalcourt ⓕ royalcourttheatre
Royal Court Theatre Sloane Square London, SW1W 8AS

The Wolf From The Door and God Bless The Child are supported by

Innovation partner

Fireworks is part of International Playwrights: A Genesis Foundation Project

 CHARITABLE FOUNDATION

ARTS COUNCIL ENGLAND
Supported using public funding by

JERWOOD CHARITABLE FOUNDATION

Jerwood New Playwrights is a longstanding partnership between the Jerwood Charitable Foundation and the Royal Court. 2014 is the 20th anniversary of the programme which supports the production of three new works by emerging writers, all of whom are in the first 10 years of their career.

The Royal Court carefully identifies playwrights whose careers would benefit from the challenge and profile of being fully produced either in the Jerwood Downstairs or Jerwood Upstairs Theatres at the Royal Court.

Since 1994, the programme has produced a collection of challenging and outspoken works which explore a variety of new forms and voices and so far has supported the production of 76 new plays. These plays include: Rachel De-lahay's **Routes**, Anders Lustgarten's **If You Don't Let Us Dream, We Won't Let You Sleep**, Suhayla El-Bushra's **Pigeons**, Clare Lizzimore's **Mint** and Alistair McDowall's **Talk Show,** Nick Payne's **Constellations**, Vivienne Franzmann's **The Witness**, E.V.Crowe's **Hero**, Anya Reiss' **Spur Of The Moment** and **The Acid Test** Penelope Skinner's **The Village Bike**, Rachel De-Lahay's **The Westbridge**, Joe Penhall's **Some Voices**, Mark Ravenhill's **Shopping And Fucking** (Co-Production With Out Of Joint), Ayub Khan Din's **East Is East** (Co-Production With Tamasha), Martin Mcdonagh's **The Beauty Queen Of Leenane** (Co-Production With Druid Theatre Company), Conor Mcpherson's **The Weir**, Nick Grosso's **Real Classy Affair**, Sarah Kane's **4.48 Psychosis**, Gary Mitchell's **The Force Of Change**, David Eldridge's **Under The Blue Sky**, David Harrower's **Presence**, Simon Stephens' **Herons**, Roy Williams' **Clubland**, Leo Butler's **Redundant**, Michael Wynne's **The People Are Friendly**, David Greig's **Outlying Islands**, Zinnie Harris' **Nightingale And Chase**, Grae Cleugh's **Fucking Games**, Rona Munro's **Iron**, Richard Bean's **Under The Whaleback**, Ché Walker's **Flesh Wound**, Roy Williams' **Fallout**, Mick Mahoney's **Food Chain**, Ayub Khan Din's **Notes On Falling Leaves**, Leo Butler's **Lucky Dog**, Simon Stephens' **Country Music**, Laura Wade's **Breathing Corpses**, debbie tucker green's **Stoning Mary**, David Eldridge's **Incomplete And Random Acts Of Kindness**, Gregory Burke's **On Tour**, Stella Feehily's **O Go My Man**, Simon Stephens' **Motortown**, Simon Farquhar's **Rainbow Kiss**, April De Angelis, Stella Feehily, Tanika Gupta, Chloe Moss And Laura Wade's **Catch**, Mike Bartlett's **My Child**, Polly Stenham's **That Face**, Alexi Kaye Campbell's **The Pride**, Fiona Evans' **Scarborough**, Levi David Addai's **Oxford Street**, Bola Agbaje's **Gone Too Far!**, Alia Bano's **Shades**, Polly Stenham's **Tusk Tusk**, Tim Crouch's **The Author**, Bola Agbaje's **Off The Endz** And DC Moore's **The Empire**.

In 2014, the 20th anniversary year of the programme, the playwrights supported are Vivienne Franzmann for **Pests**, Rory Mullarkey for **The Wolf From The Door** and Molly Davies for **God Bless The Child**.

The Jerwood Charitable Foundation is dedicated to imaginative and responsible revenue funding of the arts, supporting artists to develop and grow at important stages in their careers. It works with artists across art forms, from dance and theatre to literature, music and the visual arts.

jerwoodcharitablefoundation.org

THE ROYAL COURT THEATRE

The Royal Court is the writers' theatre. It is a leading force in world theatre, finding writers and producing new plays that are original and contemporary. The Royal Court strives to be at the centre of civic, political, domestic and international life, giving writers a home to tackle big ideas and world events and tell great stories.

The Royal Court commissions and develops an extraordinary quantity of new work, reading over 3000 scripts a year and annually producing around 14 world or UK premieres in its two auditoria at Sloane Square in London. Over 200,000 people visit the Royal Court each year and many thousands more see our work elsewhere through transfers to the West End and New York, national and international tours, residencies across London and site-specific work, including recent Theatre Local Seasons in Peckham, King's Cross and Haggerston.

The Royal Court's extensive development activity encompasses a diverse range of writers and artists and includes an ongoing programme of writers' attachments, readings, workshops and playwriting groups. Twenty years of pioneering work around the world means the Royal Court has relationships with writers on every continent.

The Royal Court opens its doors to radical thinking and provocative discussion, and to the unheard voices and free thinkers that, through their writing, change our way of seeing.

"With its groundbreaking premieres and crusading artistic directors, the Royal Court has long enjoyed a reputation as one of our most daring, seat-of-its-pants theatres."

The Times

"The most important theatre in Europe."

New York Times

Within the past sixty years, John Osborne, Arnold Wesker and Howard Brenton have all started their careers at the Court. Many others, including Caryl Churchill, Mark Ravenhill and Sarah Kane have followed. More recently, the theatre has found and fostered new writers such as Polly Stenham, Mike Bartlett, Bola Agbaje, Nick Payne and Rachel De-lahay and produced many iconic plays from Laura Wade's **Posh** to Bruce Norris' **Clybourne Park** and Jez Butterworth's **Jerusalem**. Royal Court plays from every decade are now performed on stage and taught in classrooms across the globe.

Supported using public funding by
ARTS COUNCIL ENGLAND

ROYAL COURT SUPPORTERS

The Royal Court has significant and longstanding relationships with many organisations and individuals who provide vital support. It is this support that makes possible its unique playwriting and audience development programmes.

Coutts supports Innovation at the Royal Court. The Genesis Foundation supports the Royal Court's work with International Playwrights. Theatre Local is sponsored by Bloomberg. Alix Partners support The Big Idea at the Royal Court. The Jerwood Charitable Foundation supports emerging writers through the Jerwood New Playwrights series. The Pinter Commission is given annually by his widow, Lady Antonia Fraser, to support a new commission at the Royal Court.

PUBLIC FUNDING

Arts Council England, London
British Council

CHARITABLE DONATIONS

The Austin & Hope Pilkington Charitable Trust
Martin Bowley Charitable Trust
Cowley Charitable Trust
The Dorset Foundation
The Eranda Foundation
Genesis Foundation
The Golden Bottle Trust
The Haberdashers' Company

The Idlewild Trust
Roderick & Elizabeth Jack
Jerwood Charitable Foundation
Marina Kleinwort Trust
The Andrew Lloyd Webber Foundation
John Lyon's Charity
Clare McIntyre's Bursary
The Andrew W. Mellon Foundation
The David & Elaine Potter Foundation
Rose Foundation
Royal Victoria Hall Foundation
The Sackler Trust
The Sobell Foundation
John Thaw Foundation
The Vandervell Foundation
Sir Siegmund Warburg's Voluntary Settlement
The Garfield Weston Foundation
The Wolfson Foundation

CORPORATE SUPPORTERS & SPONSORS

AKA
Alix Partners
Aqua Financial Solutions Ltd
BBC
Bloomberg
Colbert
Coutts
Fever-Tree
Gedye & Sons
Kudos Film & Television
MAC

Quintessentially Vodka
Smythson of Bond Street
White Light Ltd

BUSINESS ASSOCIATES, MEMBERS & BENEFACTORS

Annoushka
Auerbach & Steele Opticians
Byfield Consultancy
Capital MSL
Cream
Heal's
Lazard
Salamanca Group
Vanity Fair

DEVELOPMENT ADVOCATES

Elizabeth Bandeen
Anthony Burton CBE
Piers Butler
Sindy Caplan
Sarah Chappatte
Cas Donald (Vice Chair)
Celeste Fenichel
Piers Gibson
Emma Marsh (Chair)
Deborah Shaw Marquardt (Vice Chair)
Tom Siebens
Sian Westerman
Daniel Winterfeldt

Innovation partner

Supported using public funding by
ARTS COUNCIL ENGLAND

EMPLOYEES
THE ROYAL COURT & ENGLISH STAGE COMPANY

The Royal Court has been on the cutting edge of new drama for more than 50 years. Thanks to our members, we are able to undertake the vital support of writers and the development of their plays – work which is the lifeblood of the theatre.

In acknowledgement of their support, members are invited to venture beyond the stage door to share in the energy and creativity of Royal Court productions.

Please join us as a member to celebrate our shared ambition whilst helping to ensure our ongoing success.

We can't do it without you.

royalcourttheatre.com

BECOME A MEMBER

God Bless the Child

This play is dedicated to my mum,
Claire Julie Willemstyn

Thank you . . .

Everyone at the Royal Court and Dominic Cooke.

Michael and Peter Cox for building me a place to write in.

This play and I are indebted to Lyndsey Turner, who helped me research and develop the idea for a Rough Cut performance and well beyond that.

Thank you to Vicky Featherstone for wanting to put on such a play, and for never being tempted to use puppets.

Characters

Characters can be of any ethnicity, but there should be a mix.

Louie can be male or female. In the first production there were two teams of children, one with a male Louie, one with a female. For ease of reading, I have made Louie a girl in this script.

THE ADULTS

Ms Newsome, *late twenties, early thirties*
Ms Evitt, *forties*
Mrs Bradley, *early twenties or fifty-five to sixty-five*
Sali Rayner, *late forties, early fifties*
Miss Jackson, *early twenties*

THE CHILDREN OF DANDELION TABLE

Louie, *eight years old*
Grace, *eight years old*
Esther, *eight years old*
Freddie, *eight years old*
Jake, *eight years old*

THE CLASS OF 4N, INCLUDING:

Tamaya, *eight years old*
Lily Smith, *eight years old*
Aaron, *eight years old*

Badger Do Best, *a soft toy*

Setting
The play takes place in autumn over the three weeks leading up to half term. It is set in a Year 4 classroom at a primary school anywhere in the country.

There should be a fluidity/movement between scenes that reflects the primary school classroom.

Act One

One

4N, a Year Four classroom at Castlegrave Community Primary School.

There is a display of books below the prominent label SALI RAYNER'S BADGER DO BEST BOOKS. *On the wall above the display is a cuddly toy: Badger Do Best. Around him are cardboard cut-outs of other characters from Willowy Wold: Diggin Burrows, Ms Tawney Owl, Lil Harvest Mouse and Tabby Miaow.*

On another wall is a display about Henry VIII.

A large papier-mâché sun with lots of names stuck on it hangs in one corner of the classroom. In another corner hangs a rain cloud; no names are on that.

There are three stools, decorated as toadstools, in another corner.

In the middle of the room are four small tables with small chairs around them, one for each child of 4N.

Elsewhere in the classroom is a teacher's desk with a computer, an interactive whiteboard, a large stock cupboard and a floor mat painted with lilypads.

Monday afternoon. **Ms Newsome** *sits on a chair. The children are around her on the lilypad mat. Each child wears a small flip chart with a smiley face on it.*

Ms Newsome   Once upon a time, deep, deep in a willowy wood was Willowy Wold, where Badger Do Best –

She gestures to the cuddly toy Badger on the wall.

– and his friends lived peacefully. Nobody knew about these friendly creatures who shared a village in the woods. Nobody that is except . . .

Children (*whisper*)   4N.

Ms Newsome   On this particular day in Willowy Wold, the usual harmony was broken by a stomping of feet and a snapping of twigs. Diggin Burrows –

Some of the children point to the toy Diggin on the wall.

– was angry. His face was red, his fists were clenched and his heart was racing at one hundred miles an hour. He was so angry as he stomped along that he didn't even notice Badger Do Best on the other side of the path.

'Diggin!' called Badger, seeing his friend's clenched fists and furrowed brow. 'Hey, Diggin, what's wrong?'

Poor Diggin could hardly speak through his anger. 'What's wrong?' he cried. 'Don't you mean what's right?' Diggin Burrows explained to Badger that he had been building a tunnel under the woods. It had to be finished by the end of the day because his entire family was coming to stay. Diggin had been working very hard and was nearly finished when suddenly there was a big crash and his tunnel caved in. He made his way outside in time to see that the damage had been caused by Tabby Miaow chasing a worm.

'That Tabby Miaow,' said Diggin. 'I'll pull his tail, I'll throw him in the stream, I'll –'

Badger stopped him. 'You can't do that. I'm sure it was an accident, you know how Tabby gets overexcited when he's playing.'

Jake *puts up his hand.*

Ms Newsome   But Diggin refused to give up his search for Tabby Miaow, so Badger continued along the path with him, worried his friend might get into trouble. They soon came across Ms Tawney Owl.

'Oh Diggin, you don't look happy,' said clever Ms Tawney.

Diggin Burrows explained what had happened.

Jake *waves his hand around.*

Ms Newsome   'Where will my family stay now?' he asked. Hand down, please, Jake.

Jake *puts his hand down.*

Ms Newsome   'That Tabby Miaow! I'll pull his tail, I'll throw him in the stream, I'll –'

Suddenly, a tiny head poked out of the hollow of a nearby tree. It belonged to Lil Harvest Mouse.

'Please be quiet,' whispered Lil Mouse. 'I was having the loveliest dream before you woke me.' Then she saw Diggin's face. 'Oh my,' she whispered. 'What's happened?'

Jake'*s hand goes up again.*

Ms Newsome   Do you need to sit on a Thinking Toadstool?

Jake *shakes his head.*

Ms Newsome   Hand down, then.

Jake *puts his hand down. He changes his flipchart to the sad face.*

Ms Newsome   'It's that Tabby Miaow,' cried Diggin. 'I'll pull his tail, I'll throw him in the stream, I'll –'

'Stop!' exclaimed Badger Do Best. 'Diggin Burrows, you've said that over and over today. Think how much of your tunnel we could have built in that time.'

Diggin Burrows stopped. The redness drained from his face. His fists unclenched and his heart was no longer beating in his ears.

'Oh Badger, you're right,' he sighed. 'I've wasted a whole day instead of concentrating on the one thing I really wanted to achieve. My family will arrive with nowhere to stay and it's all my fault.'

'But the day's not over yet!' said Badger. 'There's always time to turn it around!'

'It's too late to get my tunnel finished now,' cried Diggin.

'Diggin Burrows, you are the hardest working creature I know,' declared Badger. 'I'll help. We've got to at least give it a try.'

'We'll help too,' cried Ms Tawney Owl and Lil Harvest Mouse.

So the friends built a tunnel, finishing just in time for the arrival of Diggin's nieces and nephews and cousins and second cousins.

And that was how Badger Do Best taught his friends that . . .

Children   It's never too late to turn the day around.

Ms Newsome *closes the book.*

Well done for doing such excellent listening, 4N.

There is a murmur among the children.

Remember you are still on the lily pads so I shouldn't have to raise my voice.

She waits.

Thank you, Tamaya. Who would like to lead us in our song before home time?

Several hands go up.

Grace, could you, please.

Lily Smith   Ms Newsome –

Ms Newsome   No questions now, Lily.

Lily Smith   Jake's crying.

Ms Newsome   Oh dear, Jake. What's up?

Jake   My mum wanted me to ask a question but I forgot and now I just remembered.

Ms Newsome Is it a very important one?

Jake Yes.

Ms Newsome Let's hear it then, quickly.

Jake When the writer Sali Rayner comes will she do a picture with us if we bring cameras and are we allowed?

Ms Newsome That's hardly an urgent question, but yes, I'm sure you can have a picture taken with Sali Rayner if you ask politely. As for cameras, you may bring them, but no expensive ones, please. I'll need to see a permission slip before you're allowed to be in any photos and cameras will have to go to Mrs Bradley at lunch time, we don't want them lying around unattended.

Lots of other hands fly up.

Ms Newsome No more questions. Anything important, ask me in the playground. Grace, thank you for waiting so patiently. Will you lead us in our song please.

Grace (*sings*)
This is our school

Children (*sing*)
It's a peaceful place
And a home to you and me
Where we are free to learn
Grow and prosper happily.

Each one of us is as unique
As snowflakes that fall from the sky.
And whatever our strengths may be
We'll try our best,
Just like Badger Do Best
And treat each other respectfully.

Pause.

Quiet.

Ms Newsome   Would Dandelion Table please quickly and quietly collect their bags and coats and stand behind their chairs.

Some of the children get up.

Could Clover do the same, please.

Some more children get up.

Foxglove and Buttercup, you can also get your things ready.

The rest of the children get up.

Quickly, Esther, you don't want to be late. Those who are ready, come down to the playground with me now. Everybody else, get a move on!

*The children, coats half-on, books falling out of their bags, follow **Ms Newsome**.*

*Except **Louie**, who is having trouble fitting a book into her bag.*

Badger Do Best   This is the story of a girl who wanted to change the world. When she was small and her parents told her if she was good she would get a sweet, the girl knew it was not true. Getting the sweet had nothing to do with being good.

Louie *manages to get the book into her bag and runs out after the others.*

Two

Tuesday afternoon. On the whiteboard are Googled images of portraits of the wives of Henry VIII. The children sit at their tables, painting.

Ms Newsome *claps a rhythm. The children stop what they are doing, clap in response and are silent.*

Ms Newsome   Is there a problem, Dandelion Table?

Freddie   She scratched me.

Grace   Freddie stole one of my paints.

Ms Newsome   What about sharing, Grace?

Grace   But he just took. You can't share if someone just takes.

Freddie   I was borrowing. She scratched, which is worse.

Ms Newsome   OK, enough. I think we need a Badger Do Best Resolution. Whose turn is it? (*Checks a list on her desk.*) Louie, could you get Badger, please.

Louie *drags her feet as she gets Badger Do Best down off the display.*

Ms Newsome   Come on!

She manoeuvres **Louie**, *who holds Badger, into position between* **Grace** *and* **Freddie**.

Ms Newsome   Ready?

Silence.

Tamaya (*whispers*)   'Let's see if we can make friends.'

Ms Newsome   Don't tell her, Tamaya. Louie, you haven't been Badger before, have you? Would you like me to do his voice with you?

Louie   I know how to do it.

Ms Newsome   Come on, then. You're keeping us all waiting.

Louie (*as Badger*)   Let's see if we can make friends. Grace, you should say how you feel about the argument.

Grace   I feel sad and also a little bit angry. I was doing Katherine Parr's face so I needed the pastel pink, and because I was in a hurry and a rush I didn't see that his hand was trying to steal it.

Freddie   You scratched.

Louie (*as Badger*)   You can talk in a minute, Freddie.

Grace   Anyway, it was an accident. But it was my paint.

Louie (*as Badger*)   And how do you feel, Freddie?

Freddie   Very very angry. This is what happened: she grabbed the pastel-pink paint out of my hand and her fingernails are scratchy and she didn't even say sorry.

Louie (*as Badger*)   Well done for sharing how you feel, Grace and Freddie. What would you do differently next time, Grace?

Grace   I would look better, then my fingernail wouldn't accidently touch him.

Louie (*as Badger*)   What would you do differently, Freddie?

Freddie   I would ask to borrow.

Louie (*as Badger*)   Is there anything else you'd both like to say?

Grace   Sorry, Freddie.

Freddie   Sorry, Grace.

Louie (*as Badger*)   Now you can shake hands.

Grace *and* **Freddie** *shake hands.*

Louie (*as Badger*)   I am very proud of you for doing your best.

Ms Newsome   Great. Well done, you three. Right, let's get back on with –

Louie (*as Badger, deviating from script*)   Shake my hand now.

Ms Newsome   Time to put Badger away.

Louie   Badger's a weak hunt.

Pause.

Ms Newsome   Name off the sunshine.

Louie   Why?

Ms Newsome   Now please, Louie.

Louie   But why?

Ms Newsome   I think you know why.

Louie   I was just saying he's going on a bear hunt, but he's catching the weak ones instead cos he wants them all to be doing their best.

Three

After school hours, the same day. The children's paintings from Scene Two are pegged up to dry.

Ms Newsome *sits at her desk, marking work and eating an edamame salad.*

Ms Evitt *enters, smartly dressed with plastic shoe-covers over her heeled shoes.*

Ms Evitt   Lydia!

Ms Newsome   Hello.

Ms Evitt *takes the bags off her shoes and puts them in the bin.*

Ms Evitt   Not got long, I'm afraid.

Ms Newsome   That's OK. How's it looking?

Ms Evitt (*picking bits of sawdust out of her hair*)   Oh. Same as three months ago: a mess. I've just been taking a group of new builders around, Jade is trying to find a cheaper deal than the people who did the first half of it. Best thing I've done this year, sending her on that procurement course. We should have all the quotes by the end of next week. Don't want to jump the gun, but it is very exciting.

Ms Newsome   Yes.

Ms Evitt   So fingers crossed for phase two of Badger Do Best.

Ms Newsome   Fingers crossed.

Ms Evitt   No pressure!

They laugh.

Before I forget, it isn't your turn to stack the dishwasher, is it?

Ms Newsome   No.

Ms Evitt   Apparently the rota's gone AWOL , there are no clean mugs down there. You can cut the tension with a knife.

Ms Newsome   I can imagine.

Ms Evitt   Everyone's blaming Rosie for some reason.

Ms Newsome   She often misses her turn.

Ms Evitt   Ah.

Ms Newsome   I'm sure it's accidental.

Ms Evitt   Yes. What wonderful art work.

Ms Newsome   Isn't it?

Ms Evitt   Clever me, employing a former artist!

Ms Newsome   Graphic designer.

Ms Evitt   They really are lovely.

Ms Newsome   It's quite easy, actually.

Ms Evitt   You should definitely display them for the assessment.

Ms Newsome   Oh, good idea.

Ms Evitt   So. What do you want?

Ms Newsome   Well, I'm sure it's nothing –

Ms Evitt   OK.

Ms Newsome   I just wanted to give you a heads-up that there may be a complaint.

Ms Evitt   Right.

Ms Newsome   From Louie Saunders' mum. She's not one for kicking up a fuss, so hopefully it won't be a problem

Ms Evitt   But . . . ?

Ms Newsome   Louie was being really –

Ms Evitt   Remind me of Louie.

Ms Newsome   She sits on Dandelion Table. Straight, dark hair?

Ms Evitt   Can't picture her . . .

Ms Newsome   Her sister Hannah is in 6R?

Ms Evitt   Right. Got her.

Ms Newsome   She messed around when being Badger in a conflict resolution so I got her to clean the paint brushes during storytime. She wasn't supposed to, but she carried on cleaning them into home time, which meant Mum couldn't find her in the playground and they missed a dentist appointment.

Ms Evitt   I imagine it'll blow over.

Ms Newsome   That's what I thought.

Ms Evitt   Cleaning paint brushes during storytime doesn't sound like a Sali Rayner technique.

Pause.

Ms Newsome   It's not exactly.

Ms Evitt   No. It's not progressive, it's not modern.

Ms Newsome   But on the course she didn't cover what to do if a child mucks about while *being* Badger.

Ms Evitt   We can't have the pilot assurance team come at half-term to assess how well Sali Rayner's system is doing only to find you are aren't even using her techniques.

Ms Newsome   But because she was actually being Badger when she messed around, I felt she should do something a bit more than sit on a toadstool. I couldn't just leave it.

Ms Evitt   So then you log the incident, don't you, in the book. Isn't that the procedure? Note down the behaviour and the fact that none of the given techniques seemed appropriate. We need to stick to the system.

Ms Newsome   I know.

Ms Evitt   We have to stick to it exactly, Lydia. Just for this phase. Just until half-term. Then it can be something Sali looks at when she makes modifications. It's not you being assessed, remember, it's the system.

Ms Newsome   Yes.

Ms Evitt   Right, I've got Deborah and Mel next.

Ms Newsome   Eek, Year Six.

Ms Evitt   Eek indeed. And my Ocado man's due at five, but they always come bloody early.

Ms Newsome   Go, go.

Four

Wednesday morning. The children sit at their tables, reading silently while **Ms Newsome** *takes the register.*

Ms Newsome (*sings*)   Hello Aaron, good morning to you.

Aaron (*sings*)   Good morning, Ms Newsome.

Ms Newsome (*sings*)   Hello Lily, good morning to you.

Lily Smith (*sings*)   Good morning, Ms Newsome.

Ms Newsome (*sings*)   Hello Tamaya, good morning to you.

Tamaya (*sings*)   Good morning, Ms Newsome.

Ms Newsome (*sings*)   Hello Freddie, good morning to you.

Freddie (*sings*)   Good morning, Ms Newsome.

Ms Newsome (*sings*)   Hello Louie, good –

Louie (*sings in tune to the Badger song*)
    This is our school
    It's a poo-y place

The rest of the children laugh, shocked.

Ms Newsome   Louie –

Ms Newsome	**Louie** (*sings loudly*)
Would Badger think	And a home to poo and pee
you're doing your best?	Where Badger's free to roam
	Poo and pee pee happily.

Ms Newsome	**Louie** (*sings, increasing in volume*)
OK, Louie. Toadstool.	Each one of us is like a freak
Now.	Poo poo pee that falls from the sky.
	But no one is the strength of me,
Louie!	We'll beat the rest,
	Even Badger Do Best,
Louie!	And treat each other nastifully.

The class erupts, with some children repeating bits of the song.

Ms Newsome   4N, ENOUGH!

The children are silent.

Five

That lunchtime. **Louie**, **Esther** *and* **Freddie** *sit on the toadstools in silence.*

Mrs Bradley *enters.*

Mrs Bradley   What naughty toe-rags have I got in 4N today, then? Esther. Freddie. Louie. Lord save me, it's the vilest 'orriblest children in the whole school.

Esther   That isn't true.

Mrs Bradley   Course it's not. I was pulling your leg, wasn't I. What's your crime?

Esther   Huh?

Mrs Bradley   What are you in for? Why have you got detention?

Freddie   This isn't detention. It's where you just sit and think about your actions on the toadstool.

Mrs Bradley   Well, whatever they're calling it this week.

Esther   Thinking Toadstool Time.

Mrs Bradley   That's detention in my book. Alright. Freddie, let me guess, you took something that wasn't yours?

Esther   He took Lily Smith's best sharpener and wouldn't give it back.

Freddie   I asked but she didn't hear.

Mrs Bradley   Then I'm not surprised you're sitting on a toadstool. Always assuming what's everyone else's is yours, it's spoilt, that is.

Esther   I put three rubbers up my nose.

Mrs Bradley   Three?

Esther   Want to see?

Mrs Bradley   They're not still up there?

Esther   No, but I can do you a demo.

Mrs Bradley   No no no. Though I am tempted, cos I've never heard of such a thing. But it's dangerous, Esther. You shouldn't do it again. (*To* **Louie**.) What about you then, missus.

Louie   I made up a song.

Mrs Bradley   You must've done more than that, you don't get told off for making up a song.

Esther   It was about Badger.

Louie   Shall I sing it to you?

Freddie   It's funny.

Mrs Bradley   I don't wanna hear if there's any bad words in it.

Louie   There's no bad words.

Freddie   There sort of is, that's how you got in trouble before.

Louie   But Ms Newsome hasn't got humour and Mrs Bradley has, so she'll like it. Shall I do it?

Mrs Bradley   Go on then.

Louie *sings.* **Esther** *and* **Freddie** *join in with the bits they remember.*

Louie (*sings*)
    This is our school
    It's a poo-y place
    And a home to poo and pee
    Where Badger's free to roam
    Poo and pee pee happily.

    Each one of us is like a freak
    Poo poo pee that falls from the sky.

But no one is the strength of me,
We'll beat the rest,
Even Badger Do Best,
And treat each other nastifully.

Esther   It's funny, isn't it?

Mrs Bradley   It is quite funny, I'll give you that.

Louie   I could teach it to you?

Esther   Yeah, let's all learn it.

Mrs Bradley   Oh no, I've got a terrible singing voice.

Freddie   I know most of it already.

Esther   I want to learn, definitely.

Louie (*to* **Mrs Bradley**)   Then if everyone else is all singing it in the playground, you can join in too.

Mrs Bradley   Alright, give us a lesson. But I'm not doing it on my own.

Louie (*sings*)
This is our school
It's a poo-y place
And a home to poo and pee –

Mrs Bradley/Louie/Esther/Freddie (*sing*)
This is our school
It's a poo-y place
And a home to poo and pee –

Louie (*sings*)
Where Badger's free to roam,
Poo and pee pee happily.

Mrs Bradley/Louie/Esther/Freddie (*sing*)
Where Badger's free to roam,
Poo and pee pee happily.

Ms Newsome *enters*.

Mrs Bradley   Right, come on, you lot, enough messing around, Ms Newsome's here now.

Ms Newsome   I hope you three are managing to do some quiet thinking?

Mrs Bradley   They were getting on really well, Miss. Then I came in and it all became too much fun, I'm afraid.

Louie   Mrs Bradley wanted to learn my song.

Mrs Bradley   Just a bit of a giggle, isn't it?

Ms Newsome   Not in the middle of class-time it's not.

Mrs Bradley   You never told me you sang it in class, you cheeky monkey.

Ms Newsome   Yes. It really distracted the rest of 4N, actually.

Louie   It didn't distract them, it made them laugh.

Ms Newsome   Louie.

Louie   Yes, Ms Newsome?

Ms Newsome   You can all go to lunch now.

The children leave.

Mrs Bradley   Funny that, her playing up. She's always been alright for me.

Ms Newsome   That's nice.

Mrs Bradley   We just seem to understand each other, I reckon.

Silence.

Mrs Bradley   You look terrible, Miss.

Ms Newsome   Thanks.

Mrs Bradley   You're not letting this test thing at half-term stress you out, are you?

Ms Newsome   No. It's not actually an assessment of me, thankfully. It's to assess the Badger system – remember from my talk?

Mrs Bradley   That's right.

Ms Newsome   And Sali Rayner herself is going to be joining us next week, so she can sort out any problems before the assurance officers arrive. Not that there really are any problems.

Mrs Bradley   If you think it's needed, I can always help out next week in class? Just in case.

Ms Newsome   That would be lovely but I doubt the budget would stretch to it.

Mrs Bradley   As it's important, though

Ms Newsome   I mean, that's why Verena was so keen to get us on this pilot in the first place, isn't it? Our lack of funds.

Mrs Bradley   But you'll have more chance of getting the funding if –

Ms Newsome   Sali Rayner does stipulate the teacher should be the only adult in the classroom.

Mrs Bradley   Sounds like it is a bit of a test of you though, Miss.

Ms Newsome   It's really not.

Mrs Bradley   Cos you've got to make a system that don't work look good.

Ms Newsome   I think it's quite hard to say whether it works or not when you aren't in my classroom during lessons.

Mrs Bradley   But I see your kids in the playground, when they're at their most real. And they're no different to any other class. Except now they're all obsessed with woodland creatures.

Ms Newsome   Well, I guess we'll let the assurance officers decide that. Sorry, Mrs Bradley, I've got so much to do here.

Mrs Bradley   Of course. (*As she's leaving.*) Miss, aren't you the music co-ordinator?

Ms Newsome   Yes.

Mrs Bradley   Then shouldn't you be encouraging song-writing?

Six

Later that day, after school hours.

Ms Newsome *eats from a bag of fruit and nuts.*

Ms Evitt   The song?

Ms Newsome   It's just not working for us.

Ms Evitt   I'm not sure that's anything worth telling Sali about.

Ms Newsome   But it's a Badger Do Best staple. We've been singing it twice a day for six weeks and it's no longer effective. In fact it's becoming a distraction. Surely she'll want to write something new before the half-term assessment?

Ms Evitt   I don't think so, no.

Ms Newsome   But I went on the course, Verena. Sali did say if there were any queries we should talk to her.

Ms Evitt   That's what she *said*. But do you think she really meant it? She'd be absolutely overwhelmed if all three head teachers came to her with every little –

Ms Newsome   But what I'm saying is, it's not a little thing.

Ms Evitt   Exactly. It's not a little thing, it's not a query.
When Sali comes next week she's expecting to check in with
us, make the occasional tweak. Because that's all that is
supposed to happen in stage one, the testing stage. Come on,
Lydia, you know this better than me: the modifications take
place in the holidays, between phases one and two. That's
when Sali will go through all the log books. All we should be
doing now is following the strategies set out. They can't
judge a system if we modify it ourselves before assessment.

Ms Newsome   If I was Sali Rayner I think I'd want to
know.

Ms Evitt   But you're not Sali Rayner. You're a brilliant
and conscientious Year Four teacher working in a school
with one hall which acts as a canteen, gym, library and
overspill from a Year Two classroom. And half an extension.
Just imagine the practical difference – as well as the
difference to morale – completing the building will make.

Silence.

Lydia, you saw the hoops they made me jump through
even to be considered for this pilot. It was like being on *The
X Factor*, and we're through to the final. Which school is
Sali Rayner likely to move forward with – the one that's
constantly tugging at her sleeve, bleating every little query
at her, or the one that quietly gets on with it? Because I can
tell you now, there is absolutely no way any of those other
heads on the scheme will be phoning up, presenting problems
and making work for everyone. Not on your nelly. They'll
be brushing it all neatly under the carpet. Because they want
that phase-two money as much as us. They need it as much
as we do. I try to protect you staff because it would be very,
very difficult going into a classroom every morning knowing
exactly how the matrix works. But you must understand it's
cut-throat out there.

Ms Newsome   Of course.

Ms Evitt   And we may not get the chance again to
improve our situation. It is frustrating. Don't think I
know that, or that I don't appreciate everything you'
doing. But somebody has to get that money – why ca
be us? We work hard enough, don't we?

Ms Newsome   We do.

Ms Evitt   What I suggest is, you log your problems with
the song, I'm sure it will have resolved itself by next week
but if not, we'll have a think about mentioning it to Sali.
How does that sound?

Ms Newsome   Fine. That sounds fine.

Seven

Thursday lunchtime. **Louie**, **Freddie**, **Grace**, **Jake** *and*
Esther *are doing chores.*

*The children unpeg the class's paintings and sort them, a different pile
for each wife of Henry VIII.*

Esther   This is a good one.

Grace   Esther, hurry.

Esther   Lily Smith did it. She's so talented at art.

Grace   We'll never get out to play with you going so slow.

Freddie   Hang on. All the Catherine of Aragons are
supposed to be together. Someone's getting it mixed up.

Grace   Probably Louie.

Louie   No.

Grace   I'm missing chess club as we speak cos of you.

Freddie   And it's a repeat offence because we sang it
twice.

Grace Exactly, so Badger makes us do this for a *week*.

Jake It's everyone's fault really, not just Louie's.

Esther I like it, anyway, I just pretend I'm a teacher.

Grace God, I'm so stressed.

Jake It's like that Badger Do Best story when they can only get across the stream if everyone paddles but Tabby Miaow gives up cos it's boring.

Grace How?

Freddie Oh yeah, then Lil Harvest Mouse gives up –

Jake All of them do –

Freddie And then they sink –

Jake And they realised they sinked cos there was a tiny hole and they would've been fine only no one paddled and they all blame Tabby Miaow.

Esther So mean.

Grace I don't get how that's like –

Freddie And Badger says we can't blame Tabby because we all need to take responsibility –

Jake See, like Grace blaming Louie for making up the song. We all singed so we all have to take responsibility.

Grace They didn't sink though, in the story.

Freddie They did.

Esther No, they all swam, remember, cos then they helped pull Diggin Burrows out.

Grace Thank you!

Freddie Diggin wasn't even there, you mean the one where they did teamwork

Grace   As if they'd drown anyway. What about all the stories that came after?

Freddie   I didn't say they drowned, I said the boat sinked.

Grace   Then how did it end?

Esther   Is it when Badger shows them good sharing?

Grace   No.

Jake *roots through the Badger Do Best book display.*

Louie   Why are you even arguing for, they're all the same anyway.

Jake   They're not.

Louie   That's why no one can remember.

Esther   Don't be silly, Louie.

Louie   Badger does his best and somebody learns a lesson.

Freddie   But all the stuff they learn is different, that's why there's different stories, stupid.

Jake   'Badger and the Rowing Boat', it's called. 'Badger and the Rowing Boat'.

Freddie   Look at the end

Grace   See who's right

Jake   OK. 'The three friends swapped positions until they finally –'

Louie *takes the book off* **Jake** *and tears out the page.*

Jake   Louie!

Esther   Louie, books are sacred!

Jake   You are going to be on the rain cloud for a long, long time.

Grace   Forever.

Freddie   You'll definitely get a letter home.

Esther   You've *ruined a book*.

Louie   No, I'm making it better. It had a rubbish ending. I can do a good one.

Grace   Do it, then.

Louie   What happened is:

> The animals were in the boat and
> the water was all going up their noses and
> into their mouths and their eyeballs and –
> just as they were about to die away –
> they heard something amazing.
> They looked up and it was
> The King.

Grace   What King?

Louie

> She looked like me and her name was Louie
> only she was a King.
> King Louie said 'Let's swim,'
> but the animals didn't have life jackets,
> Badger had forgot to pack them.
> So King Louie
> put her hand over Badger's mouth.
> 'Diggin, blow in Badger's ear,' she said.
> Lil Harvest Mouse blowed in the other ear.
> King Louie blowed up his nose.
> They blowed and blowed
> till they had no blow left
> and Badger was a
> big
> fat
> floatable.

> 'Weeee,' they went as they jumped into the river,
> holding on to Badger's arms and legs.

'Swim, Badger,' they were all shouting,
'Come on, Badger Do Best, do your best.'
They shouted
'DO YOUR BEST'
till they got to the other side and they were all
safe and dry.

Grace   Then what about Badger, did he –

Louie   Then to make Badger be back to normal, all the animals sat on him. And all the air whizzed out of him like *pppbbff*.

Grace, **Esther**, **Jake** *and* **Freddie** *laugh and blow raspberries too.*

Mrs Bradley *enters.*

Mrs Bradley   This don't look much like doing chores to me.

Jake   A page of a book just fell out.

Mrs Bradley   Ah.

Louie   It doesn't matter though, it's only from a Badger Do Best story, and they're rubbish.

Mrs Bradley *looks at the children.*

Jake   It was an accident.

Mrs Bradley   Was it indeed.

She takes the book and the ripped-out page over to **Ms Newsome**'s *desk.*

Esther   What's going to happen?

Mrs Bradley   Tell you what's going to happen. You lot are going to get on with what you're supposed to be doing and I'm going to stick this page back in and we'll say no more about it. (*Holds the book out.*) See, good as new. Jake, put the book back where it lives.

Bless the Child

love you, Mrs Bradley.

ey   I bet you do. When I come back, I want
gs all sorted. Alright?

...ight.

Mrs Bradley *leaves.*

Louie   See, even Mrs Bradley thinks Badger Do Best is a idiot.

Esther   'Come on Badger, do your best!'

Grace   That was actually a good ending, Louie.

Freddie   *Pppbbff!*

They all laugh.

Eight

Louie
   The maggots had
   wrinkled, purpley see-through
   skin
   and shivered like they were cold.
   Badger said, 'Eat up,'
   and everyone did
   because of politeness.
   Lucky Esther:
   she was only allowed to eat
   raw food vegetables and grains by her mum,
   so she had a lunch box.

   The next bit is:

   Badger Do Best opened his mouth and
   the disgustingest smell
   and colour
   shot greeny yellow

down Lil Mouse's face.
Badger
burped
and a maggot crawled out of his mouth.

Esther (*impressed*)   You're disgusting.

Louie
Her diary was
heavy with busy timetables.
BASH!
She hit Badger
round the head with it
and his brains
exploded.
Then everyone cheered
brave Grace
and said she was
the greatest.

Grace   Yay, me!

Louie
Jake was best at hiding cos
he was used to standing
still as a statue,
not moving a muscle,
in photos.
He ranned out from
behind a tree and
Badger jumped a hundred metres high and
screamed
and weed his pants.

The children laugh.

Louie
Badger Do Best snarled,
'My dad is going to kill you,'
and Daddy Badger's teeth were

all pointy and his claws
all sharp.
But, ha ha, what Badger didn't know was
Freddie was ruler of the daddies;
dads just said yes whatever he wanted.
So Freddie said, 'Stop showing me your teeth,'
and the Daddy Badger stopped.
Freddie said, 'Put your claws away,'
and the Daddy Badger did.
And then Clever Freddie had a idea:
he said
'Now I want you to kill your son.'

Nine

Friday lunchtime.

Mrs Bradley *and the whole of 4N are drenched.*

Esther   It's not fair, though.

Grace   It's not natural to be all cooped up.

Mrs Bradley   Don't need to tell me. Bit of rain never
hurt no one, I say, but you know how health and safety is.

Grace   Please, Mrs Bradley –

Esther   We'll love you forever?

Mrs Bradley   Stop your whining, you two. Who's wet
play monitor?

Tamaya   I'm the Badger Buddy.

Mrs Bradley   Right, get out the CD then, Tamaya.

Aaron   Oh, not the CD, please not the CD.

Lily Smith   Can I be Badger, please Mrs Bradley?

Mrs Bradley   Seeing as you asked so nicely.

Lily Smith *gets Badger down from his display.*

Mrs Bradley   Alright then, all of you, find a space. Jake, quiet a minute. I don't wanna be inside any more than you lot, but we're stuck with it, so let's make the most of a bad situation and get a little bit of exercise, alright? Hurry up, Tamaya, cos I've gotta check on Year Three in a minute. Lily Smith, you got the Badger?

Lily Smith   Here.

Mrs Bradley   Alright, Tamaya, press play.

Lily Smith *stands at the front of the class with Badger, moving him in time with the CD.*

Voice on CD   Take a walk through Willowy Wold with me.

The children walk on the spot.

There's Diggin Burrows, give him a wave.

They wave.

Let's climb a tree.

They 'climb'.

And jump in the stream

They jump.

Careful!

Louie *joins in with the CD, shouting so that her voice is louder.*

Oooh, it's terribly chilly –

They 'shiver'.

Now swim!

They 'swim'.

There's Lil Mouse, let's wave!

They wave while swimming.

Careful!

Louie *pushes* **Lily Smith** *and Badger to one side and climbs on a table. She shouts her own instructions over the top of the tape.*

Louie   Let's climb a chair.

The children all climb on to chairs.

There's Tabby Miaow, stick your fingers up.	**Mrs Bradley** Right, off there. Come on, you lot.

They do.

Bow to your king.

They do.

Say 'King Louie'.

Children   King Louie.

Mrs Bradley   Ms Newsome won't be very –

Louie   Say 'King Louie'!

Children King Louie!	**Mrs Bradley** King Louie! I mean –

Louie (*jumping up and down on the table*)   SAY 'KING LOUIE'!

Children (*bowing/jumping*)   KING LOUIE!

Louie *strikes a pose like Henry VIII on the wall display.*

The children jump around on the tables and chairs shouting 'King Louie'.

Ms Newsome *enters.*

Ms Newsome   4N!

The children stop. They climb off chairs etc.

Mrs Bradley, could you take the children to the hall to choose library books, please. Louie, I'd like you to stay here.

Mrs Bradley *and 4N exit.*

Ms Newsome   I'm not going to tell you off. I just wanted to find out what's going on at the moment.

Louie   I'm doing my best.

Ms Newsome   Yes. But is there anything you want to talk about?

Louie   No.

She exits.

Act Two

One

Louie *sits on* **Ms Newsome**'s *chair. The children sit around her on the lily pad mat.*

Louie   Once upon a time, deep, deep in a willowy wood was Willowy Wold, where Badger Do Best and his friends lived peacefully. Nobody knows about these friendly creatures who share a village in the wood, nobody that is except –

Children (*shout*)   4N.

Louie   Particularly this day,
4N
waked up from a dream
where they'd all had the
same dream,
which was
Badger Do Best was just a
lie
held together with stitches.
4N thought,
'The dream's probably not real.'
But they kept having
second doubts
so
one brave girl
decided to find out.

When Badger was talking to her about
moving around school quietly and carefully,
the girl
quietly
and carefully
feeled along Badger's neck till she got a

little stitch sticking out.
She pinched the stitch
between her fingers and
pulled until it
pulled out.
Then 4N pulled
more and more stitches, till Badger got
beheaded
into tiny pieces.
Then they used all those
tiny pieces of Badger
to staple all together to make a
crown
and they put it on the
brave girl's head
and they
shouted:

Children   King Louie! King Louie! King Louie!

Two

Monday, after school hours. **Ms Newsome** *eats a packet of cheese and onion crisps.*

Badger is on the floor.

Ms Evitt *enters.*

Ms Evitt   Just a quick one. (*Seeing Badger.*) Oh dear. (*She puts him on a table.*) Mel's on the warpath. Something about a display board in the hall.

Ms Newsome   Year Six can't hog all the boards. We don't have enough space, what with all the Badger paraphernalia.

Ms Evitt   I'm not getting involved, just thought I'd warn you as I'm passing by.

Ms Newsome   I did get permission from Rosie. Surely it's up to her, as display coordinator.

Ms Evitt   Yes, but she misunderstood what you asked, apparently.

Ms Newsome   Because Mel put the pressure on. Great. That woman is such a bully.

Ms Evitt   Are you telling me this officially?

Ms Newsome   No.

Ms Evitt   Phew! Have a good evening, Lydia.

Ms Newsome   The Badger Do Best system isn't working.

Ms Evitt   Which part? Are you still struggling with the song?

Ms Newsome   Oh God, I can't even *attempt* the song.

Ms Evitt   You must persevere, Lydia. I thought we agreed.

Ms Newsome   The badger part isn't working.

Ms Evitt   What do you mean?

Ms Newsome   I mean, I'm banging on about Badger every day and the kids are over it. They don't care. They won't do anything he says. So I don't know what the point is in having this assessment.

Ms Evitt   The point is the funding we'll get in stage two.

Ms Newsome   They won't give us the funding if the class is uncontrollable.

Ms Evitt   I'm not sure you can blame a stuffed toy for your inability to control your class.

Ms Newsome   I can control them. Badger can't.

Ms Evitt   Can you hear yourself, Lydia?! Look, is there any child in particular you are having problems with?

Ms Newsome   Everything was fine until Badger came along.

Ms Evitt   So what do you suggest? How can I help you?

Ms Newsome   Let me talk to Sali Rayner before the assessment.

Ms Evitt   No.

Ms Newsome   When she comes on Friday, let me tell her –

Ms Evitt   What? That you can't control your class? Why would she want to keep working with us after that?

Ms Newsome   Actually, let me ask her. Let me ask her if the assurance officers will be looking at academic progress at half-term. Because there won't be any; a classroom where the child is king doesn't make for healthy results. Which is actually what Deborah and Mel said all along, dammit.

Ms Evitt   The child is not supposed to be king.

Ms Newsome   Child-led, then. A child-led classroom. Which is basically the same thing.

Ms Evitt   You absolutely cannot speak to Sali about this.

Ms Newsome   So we're sacrificing 4N's progress to get some funding?

Ms Evitt   We're not sacrificing anyone. We're adapting.

Ms Newsome   But we're adapting into something which doesn't benefit the children.

Ms Evitt   Even if 4N do have a bit of a tricky term, think what they get at the end of it. You're being very negative, Lydia. It's not like you.

Ms Newsome   I just feel like, you know, I'm the one in
the classroom, so –

Ms Evitt   You're right, you are the one in the classroom
and that does bring many challenges. But also many rewards.
You get to be part of change, of progress. We are going to
influence a scheme that might be taken on by every school
in the country. Which is something that could do a lot for
both of our futures. So let's really work on solving your
problem. We need to make Badger Do Best relevant again.
One of his stories must cover this kind of predicament, why
don't you –

Ms Newsome   They don't.

Ms Evitt   Then make one up!

Ms Newsome   But aren't I supposed to be sticking to
exactly what's in the Badger Do Best system?

Ms Evitt   Are you being deliberately obtuse? My
goodness! (*Checks watch.*) I know it's a big adjustment, Lydia,
changing not just the way you teach but also how you
discipline, how you set out your classroom – and you've
been doing a fantastic job like I knew you would. It's not
ideal, the children going off Badger at this stage in the
game, but that's what's happened. And teaching is about
having many more ways to tackle a problem than just plan B.
Have a go. Improvise, invent a story – but don't deviate
from Sali's ethos. If you manage to get them back on track,
your story might even be incorporated into the system.

Pause.

You know, I chose you to be the Badger Do Best teacher
because you're not like Deborah and Mel. You're enthusiastic
and creative and adaptable and I knew you would –

Ms Newsome   Be mug enough to take it on?

Ms Evitt   *Make it work.*

She exits.

Ms Newsome *writes 'fuck off' on the white board.*

Three

Tuesday afternoon. **Ms Newsome** *sits on a chair with the children around her on the mat.*

Ms Newsome   Once upon a time, deep, deep in a willowy wood was Willowy Wold, where Badger Do Best and his friends lived in peace and harmony. Nobody knew about those friendly creatures who shared a village in the woods. Nobody that is except . . .

Silence.

Well, this particular day in Willowy Wold, Tabby Miaow was feeling very, very angry with Badger.

The children start humming.

Tabby – stop that please – was fed up of Badger bossing him around.

The humming gets louder.

Tabby Miaow had really come to the end of his tether.

The humming gets louder still and **Ms Newsome** *increases her volume too.*

He thought, 'Next time Badger speaks –'

The children hum as loudly as possible.

'I'm not going to do what he says. In fact' – 4N. QUIET. NOW.

The children's hums become 'ahh's.

'In fact –'

Ms Newsome *gives up.*

Four

Wednesday lunchtime. The class sits at their desks.

The children have all turned their flip charts to frowning faces.

All the children's names are now on the rain cloud.

Grace   No, I have to do the writing cos I'm the only one with a pen licence.

Esther   It does look better in pen, Jake.

Jake   OK.

Freddie   Ready? Anne Boleyn speaked French because she had lived there when she was a baby.

Grace   Slowly, Freddie, I'm doing joined up.

Freddie   The next bit will be about how she had dark brown hair and all the English people hated her.

Esther   But Henry didn't hate her cos he wrote seventeen love letters to her and he put them at the Vatican.

Grace   Hang on, hang on

Jake   The important thing is: Henry VIII and Anne Boleyn got married. Write that.

Esther   Even though he was married to Catherine thing.

Jake   Do the bit about how she got a baby, too.

Freddie   Next you have to write: 'Anne Boleyn was pregnant with a baby inside.'

Louie   But unfortunately it was baby Princess Elizabeth.

Mrs Bradley *enters.*

Mrs Bradley   Oh my word. What's happened?

Tamaya   Nothing.

Mrs Bradley   Must be pretty bad for all of you to be kept in. Don't reckon I've ever seen a whole class staying behind at lunch.

Lily Smith   We only didn't want to be burned by the sun.

Aaron   The sun can kill you.

Mrs Bradley   I suppose that's true.

Lily Smith   But Ms Newsome wants us to put our names back on.

Aaron   So it's a dilemma.

Mrs Bradley   I see. Well, it does seem extreme you all being kept in, but I think Ms Newsome wants to keep everything how it should be for your visitor on Friday.

Tamaya   What?

Mrs Bradley   Pardon, young lady. You know, Sali whatsit the author.

Tamaya   Sali Rayner! She won't care about the sunshine though, she just wrote about Badger.

Mrs Bradley   Exactly, she created the Badger, she made up all the stories. And who do you reckon thought of having listening lily pads and thinking toadstools?

Aaron   Sali Rayner?

Mrs Bradley   And them textbooks you have with the Badger doing his best on the front, that's all Sali Rayner. And the names on the sun and the rain cloud and the way this whole classroom is laid out, that's her too.

Lily Smith   Sali Rayner must be really clever.

Mrs Bradley   So Ms Newsome has to make sure everything looks the way she's been taught.

Louie   Sali Rayner teached Ms Newsome?

Mrs Bradley   And Ms Evitt. Only I think Ms Evitt just did a day or something. Ms Newsome did a whole course.

Tamaya   Did you do a course?

Mrs Bradley   Lord no, I'm not important enough, but Ms Newsome did tell me about it

Esther   You're important to me, Mrs Bradley.

Louie   Sali Rayner tells Ms Evitt and Ms Newsome what to do?

Mrs Bradley   Well, someone has to, don't they? Teachers may act like they know everything, but someone always has to tell them.

Esther   When I'm a teacher, no one will tell me what to do.

Five

Thursday morning.

Ms Newsome *is standing.*

The children sit with their backs to her, instead facing **Louie**.

Ms Newsome   This is your final warning.

The children stay where they are.

Ms Newsome   I'm going to count you back, like we do in the baby classes, just in case you are having a problem understanding. At zero I want everyone back in their seats.

Silence.

Ms Newsome   Five. Four. Three. Two. One. Zero.

The children stay put.

THIS STOPS NOW.

No one moves.

Right

She makes for **Louie** *but the children stand, blocking her path.*

They face her.

Six

Lunchtime, the same day.

Ms Newsome *and* **Ms Evitt** *enter.*

Ms Evitt   You're gong to have to explain it to me like I'm stupid.

Ms Newsome (*taking a Snickers bar out of her desk*)   She's unteachable.

Ms Evitt   Of course Sali Rayner would say there's no such thing.

Ms Newsome   I'm not saying she's a lost cause, generally. I'm sure if someone were to dedicate all their time to just her, doing activities she dictated, she'd be fine. But that's not school, is it? It could be disastrous if she's in next Friday. If we could find a reason to keep her out of school for the day

Ms Evitt   Excluding children isn't very child-led.

Ms Newsome   It is if it's better for the rest of the children in the class.

Ms Evitt   We've neither suspended nor excluded a single
child since I've been at Castlegrave.

Ms Newsome   Which is impressive

Ms Evitt   It's a fact I'm very proud of, and I'm not going
to taint that record over whatever this is. Not to mention
risk our funding. It's not an option.

Ms Newsome   But keeping her in school will risk losing
the funding.

Ms Evitt   How long have you been unable to teach this
little girl?

Ms Newsome   Not long.

Ms Evitt   Because you realise of course that you are
telling me *a week before the assurance officers arrive*, that there
might be an issue.

Ms Newsome   I thought it was under control. I was
dealing with it.

Ms Evitt   Two parents of children in 4N have asked to see
me later this week, regarding their son or daughter's
involvement with another child. Is that child likely to be
Louie?

Ms Newsome   Yes.

Ms Evitt   I'm really quite upset and disappointed that you
didn't come to me the minute you had problems with her.
I've prioritised the work you've been doing on the pilot
scheme, I've made myself as available as possible, offered
support and advice

Ms Newsome   What – 'Do everything Sali Rayner
taught you,' 'Oh no, actually, make it up as you go along.'

Ms Evitt   Lydia.

Ms Newsome   What's this? (*Gestures to a toadstool.*) What
technique do you use with it? What are the three rules of the

listening lily pads? You don't know how any of this stuff works, how could you advise on it? I don't know what to do with her, I admit it. Usually I'm good with the naughty ones. I'm good with the seething-little-ball-of-anger ones. But she's different. She's calm and in control and she thinks she's the king. I don't know what she wants.

Ms Evitt   But what does she *do*?

Ms Newsome   She picks at, she unpicks, everything I do. You'd have to see it. But I need help.

Ms Evitt   Then I'll see it.

Seven

Later that afternoon, the children of 4N are at their tables as **Ms Newsome** *teaches.*

Ms Evitt *observes from the back of the class.*

Ms Newsome   Who can remember – sorry, is there a problem, Louie?

Louie   No, Ms Newsome.

Ms Newsome   Who can remember what we were looking at last time in our project work?

Hands shoot up.

Ms Newsome   Lily?

Lily Smith   We were looking about rich and poor Tudor people?

Ms Newsome   Well done for remembering, but it was actually the lesson before last we looked at poverty in the Tudor times. Who else has an idea?

Hands shoot up.

Ms Newsome   Tamaya?

Tamaya   We learned about how Henry VIII wanted to be married with Anne Boleyn.

Ms Newsome   Well done, Tamaya. We also looked at the reason he had to break away from the Catholic Church to do that. Who can remember. Louie?

Louie   Cos he needed to be the important one, not the Pope. He changed all their believes so he could do what he wants.

Pause.

Ms Newsome   Yes, OK. But there was something in particular he wanted, wasn't there?

Aaron   I know, I know: to divorce with Catherine of Aragon.

Ms Newsome   Aaron, that question was for Louie. No calling out.

Ms Evitt   My goodness! 4N, I am so impressed with how much you know about the Tudors. What a lucky class you are to have Ms Newsome who obviously helps you do such good learning. (*To* **Ms Newsome**.) I would love to stay here all afternoon, but I really must get on with the job of managing our school.

Ms Newsome   But you haven't seen anything.

Ms Evitt   Because you have it under control, my dear. You're too hard on yourself. Oh – (*Points to a display board.*) These borders are peeling a bit, aren't they?

Ms Newsome   It's probably the heating.

Ms Evitt   We should aim for immaculate next week, I think.

Ms Newsome   They'll be familiar with a working classroom though, won't they?

Ms Evitt   Who knows!

Ms Newsome   And it's the system being judged, not me?

Ms Evitt   Don't be naive, Lydia. (*To the class.*) Have a
wonderful afternoon, everybody.

Ms Evitt *exits.*

Louie *stands.*

Louie   Now King Louie will pick her husbands and wifes.

The children rush to her. **Ms Newsome** *stands to one side.*

Tamaya   I'll be the wife.

Louie   Only the strongest can be wifes.

Aaron   I bet I can lift Jake and Lily at once.

The children argue, start trying to lift one another.

Ms Newsome *calls out the door.*

Ms Newsome   Ms Evitt!

The children sit back down in their seats.

Ms Newsome   Don't you DARE. No, don't you DARE
sit there as if. (*To* **Louie**.) YOU SMUG LITTLE GIRL!

Ms Evitt *enters.*

Ms Evitt   What's going on?

Louie   Ms Newsome just started shouting.

Ms Newsome   No no no, you tell her how you behaved
as soon as she left the room. She was choosing who to
marry. TELL HER!

Ms Evitt   I think

Ms Newsome   WILL SOMEONE JUST ADMIT
WHAT'S GOING ON HERE?

Ms Evitt   Ms Newsome –

Ms Newsom   But of course none of you will, will you?
Because she's your king. Well I'm your teacher and you
have to do as I say. THAT'S HOW SCHOOL WORKS.

Ms Evitt   MS NEWSOME!

Eight

Friday morning. **Ms Evitt** *sits on* **Ms Newsome**'s *chair. The
children sit around her on the mat of lily pads.*

Ms Evitt   Once upon a time there was a woman who had
a very important job, some might say the most important
job in the world. And one day –

Grace   What was the job?

Ms Evitt   The job was. She worked at an animal park and
her job was to help prepare the animals for going into the
wild. The woman loved the animals but her job was long
and demanding and sometimes she got angry and snapped
at them. One day when she hadn't had much sleep – and
we all know how that makes us feel, don't we? Very tired
and irritable – the woman shouted at the animals and said
horrible upsetting things that she immediately regretted.
And do you know what the animals did? Did they cry? Did
they run off and tell their mums and dads? No. They dealt
with the incident in a very, very mature way. Because they
understood that sometimes we get tired and we behave in a
different manner to how we would like. So.

Aaron   Ms Evitt –

Ms Evitt   What should you do if you'd like to say
something?

Aaron *puts his hand up.*

Ms Evitt   4N, I am going to be teaching you today as
Ms Newsome has become quite tired and poorly so she's

going to be resting at home for a little while. I'm sure you will all be very mature and responsible about the situation, especially this afternoon when Sali Rayner is here. Aaron?

Aaron   Is that the end of the story?

Ms Evitt   What? Oh, sorry, yes: The End.

Nine

Later on Friday morning.

The children sit at their tables. **Mrs Bradley** *wanders the classroom, carrying Badger Do Best.*

Mrs Bradley   Hang on. Lily, you never did that yourself?

Esther   She did, Lily's really good at art.

Mrs Bradley   Shhh, Esther. Well, the Badger reckons that's the best picture he's ever seen, don't you?

She nods Badger's head.

Tamaya   You're not supposed to say someone's done *the best*. Nobody can be better than anyone else.

Mrs Bradley   Alright, bossyboots. And the Badger thinks you're doing *your* best too, Aaron. Freddie, he does not think you're doing your best. (*As Badger.*) 'If you don't shut up Freddie, I'm going to have to start calling you Freddie Do Bad.'

The children laugh.

Mrs Bradley   Jake, the Badger thinks that's fantastic. Shhh, everyone quiet except for the Badger.

Ms Evitt *enters with* **Sali Rayner**.

The children continue to work in silence.

Ms Evitt   Unfortunately Ms Newsome is off sick, so I am taking the class today, with the help of Mrs Bradley, a teaching assistant.

Mrs Bradley (*vaguely*)   Oooh, the Badger thinks that's lovely.

Sali   What a beautiful classroom.

Ms Evitt   Yes.

Sali   Oh, and you've got the toadstools over there.

Ms Evitt   I think Ms Newsome felt they worked best in the book corner.

Sali   I love that there is a certain amount of flexibility in my system, so the teacher is able to put their stamp on it. Wonderful. Wonderful.

Ms Evitt   Would you like to introduce yourself to the class? I know a few of them are keen for you to sign their books.

Sali   Of course.

Ms Evitt   Children, could you stop what you are doing and face this way, please. Thank you. As you know, we are lucky enough to have a very exciting visitor in school today. I'd like us all to listen carefully while Sali Rayner explains why she's here.

Sali   Hello, children. Thank you so much for letting me come and admire your wonderful classroom and all the brilliant work you've been doing. My name, as I'm sure most of you know, is Sali – bit of an unusual spelling, it's with an 'i' – and that's what you can call me. No formalities, no Mrs Whatnot. You might recognise me from ITV's *Classroom Capers*, or perhaps that was before your time; you may know me because your parents or teachers have my books *Unconditional Praise for Little People* or *Making Sharing Time Sparkle* but you will most definitely know my name

from the textbooks you have been studying and the
storybooks you've been enjoying at story-time. I am here
today because some lovely people from the government
asked me to find a way to help children always do their best.
And so I came up with a wonderful character, one you're all
very familiar with: Badger Do Best.

Louie   Arrgh!

She stands.

She punches Badger Do Best out of **Mrs Bradley***'s grasp.*

*She jumps on to a table, holding Badger. Takes scissors from a pencil
pot and hacks at him.*

Badger's head falls to the ground.

The children clap, shout 'King Louie'.

Blackout.

Act Three

One

Sali *sits on* **Ms Newsome**'s *chair. The children sit around her on the lily pad mat.* **Louie** *sits on a toadstool.* **Sali** *reads from a notebook.*

Sali Tabby put on Diggin's shoes and Diggin put on Tabby's shoes.

Badger Do Best and Diggin skipped ahead. Now Tabby Miaow lagged behind.

'Wait,' he begged. 'These shoes are so painful, I don't blame you for being slow, Diggin.'

So Diggin put his new shoes back on and the three friends walked on happily, together, at a much slower pace.

And that was how Badger Do Best taught Tabby Miaow to walk in somebody else's shoes.

Do you know, you are the first children ever to have heard that story. It's brand new. What do you think about that, 4N?

Silence.

Two

Monday morning.

Sali *applies hand-sanitiser.*

Ms Evitt Those parents want my blood. Or Louie's. Mostly mine, I think, for letting her behaviour get out of hand. I should've listened to Lydia. We need to exclude her.

Sali No. It was right to keep her in class.

Ms Evitt   Lydia followed Badger Do Best exactly though, and Louie didn't –

Sali   Lydia obviously had some issues of her own, from what you've said. You don't shout like that at children otherwise. I don't know her situation, but often when teachers feel a powerlessness in other parts of their life they abuse the power they have when in school.

Ms Evitt   I don't think that's Lydia.

Sali   It's easier to feel anger at children than it is with whatever is really causing you pain. I've seen it a lot. Lydia's own internal discord damaged the vision she was trying to promote to the children – that of Badger Do Best. It even affected her immune system in the end. But we needn't worry about Lydia until she's back from sick leave, our job now is to find a way of engaging Louie.

Ms Evitt   That girl.

Sali   We need to move forward, Verena. I have to work this out. If any of my three schools aren't functioning within the Badger Do Best system, the scheme fails. That means no phase two for anyone.

Ms Evitt   And how are the others doing?

Sali   Wonderfully.

Ms Evitt   God, you must rue the day you heard of Castlegrave.

Sali   Not at all. I'm an experienced practitioner, Verena. Of course I knew the Badger Do Best system we've been testing in phase one was never going to suit all children. How could it? It wasn't designed to. The idea was always that as well as solving any problems which arose in phase one, I'd create SEN provision for children with specific needs in phase two. Louie's behaviour on Friday was really interesting

Ms Evitt   That's one word for it.

Sali   Really illuminating. What I suggest is this: I'll work in isolation with Louie this week, to ensure she's defused in time for the DfE assessment. And the work I do with her will inform my phase two modifications.

Ms Evitt   You know Louie isn't statemented. She's not special

Sali   There's something special in all of us, Verena.

Ms Evitt   Of course, but –

Sali   Listen, I'm going to let you in on a bit of a secret. I know we hear a lot at the moment about attainment, about wanting to build a world-class school system etcetera. But that's actually a red herring. Because, of course, what politicians really want is to keep voters happy. And do you know what it turns out voters really want? The moral anchor of society to be restored. And for children to have good enough grammar to be understood. And not to have to worry about being stabbed whenever they step outside their door. So, a learning system that integrates behavioural targets is the holy grail. And that's exactly what my Badger Do Best system does!

Ms Evitt   And academic progress?

Sali   Oh, academic progress still matters, of course. It always will. But behaviour, behaviour is big at the moment. Behaviour is key. The Department has even indicated that, as well as being used in every state school in the country, Badger Do Best has the capability to be rolled out into the community. They say it could cross over into dealing with troubled families, and problems with unrest and anti-social behaviour. That's how keen they are!

Ms Evitt   I didn't realise it's only for state schools

Sali   Just think, there could be a time when improvement in behaviour is actually acknowledged! Verena, imagine: a time with fewer tests that need to be passed at some pulled-out-of-thin-air percentage. Wouldn't that be marvellous?

Ms Evitt   Of course.

Sali   Let's be real. We both know, don't we, that right now, no one looks at what a school really has to offer a child. No one is interested in the added value it provides. Am I wrong?

Ms Evitt   You're right.

Sali   No one honours creativity or tests the children for happiness and love. Where does it mention that when a child entered the school they were angry and violent, or needy and hurt?

Ms Evitt   Unable to sit at a table, didn't know what a knife and fork were for.

Sali   Yes. With deep rooted, emotional wounds

Ms Evitt   Or had just never heard the word 'no'. There's nowhere that says this is how they came in, and now look at them. They can sit at a table!

Sali   They are happy!

Ms Evitt   And it's not just one child sitting at a table, it's thirty. There's no acknowledgement of that. No awareness of the huge potential, the massive potential, for chaos there is in that. I mean, forget learning the names of Henry VIII's wives, it's a miracle they can sit at a table!

Sali   And this is precisely why Badger Do Best works for everyone! Because of course, if we prioritise the behavioural bit, if we get that sorted, children are then free to learn. It will be like teaching in a public school for everybody! Finding Louie really was the best thing that could've happened.

Ms Evitt   Wow. So, this incident just means you'll get a head start on the phase two modifications. It's not a disaster.

Sali   I see only silver linings.

Ms Evitt   It's not a disaster.

Sali   You look in desperate need of a Cotton Wool Moment.

Ms Evitt   That sounds amazing, whatever it is.

Sali   Listen, I need you to think of me as your fairy godmother. I have a gift – I don't know where it comes from – but I've not yet met a child who doesn't respond to me. And I've worked with children wilder than your Louie.

Ms Evitt   Oh God, the parents. I'm not sure they'll stand for Louie staying in school. They know I'd be loath to permanently exclude her, but they'll expect her to be suspended at the very least.

Sali   Why don't you put out a letter? Explain that I'll be working with Louie alone until she's ready to come back to the class. We'll need to detail how exactly they should speak to their children about her. This has to be a shared vision, school and home united.

Ms Evitt   Right.

Sali   I'll take sessions with the rest of the class too, that should reassure them. And mention that I've already shared with their children a new, as yet unpublished Badger Do Best story.

Ms Evitt   Right. OK. I'll have Jade get an email out.

Sali   Great, then I can send you over some links to include – one to my website and another to a talk that someone put on YouTube. Might be useful. But first things first, grab that Cotton Wool Moment. Not sure the name quite conveys the meaning. It'll be in my next book. It's about taking that much-needed me-time, allowing yourself that. It should feel soft and warm and like it protects you, as if you were wrapped in cotton wool. Let's try it, I'd love your feedback. Do you have any biscuits?

Three

That afternoon, **Louie** *sits on* **Ms Newsome**'s *chair, spinning herself around.* **Sali** *sits on a child's chair.*

Sali   Louie.

Silence.

Louie.

Louie   *King* Louie.

Sali   Of course. Well, King Louie, I gather you like to tell stories. Is that right?

Silence.

Is that right?

Silence.

Louie?

Louie   You have to bow.

Sali   Bow?

Louie   If you want to talk to me.

Sali   Well, this is fun.

She bows elaborately.

King Louie! May I speak with you, Your Majesty?

Louie   You have to wait until I say no or yes after you say King Louie. Then you can speak what you want to say.

Sali   Right. OK. King Louie!

Silence.

King Louie! Can't you hear me, Your Majesty?

Louie   You forgot.

Sali   Huh?

Louie   You forgot to bow.

Sali   Oh yes. Silly me. Right. (*She bows.*) King Louie!

Pause.

Louie   Yes?

Sali   May I speak with you a while?

Louie   Only if you don't do that stupid voice.

Sali   I'm not doing a –

OK. How's this – I'd like to talk to you for a bit, King Louie.

Louie   You have to ask to speak again. Bow and say King Louie and everything.

Sali *pulls up the child's chair next to* **Louie**.

Sali   Sorry, matey, I wasn't born yesterday. We could go on like this for ever.

Silence

If you won't speak to me then I shall just have to speak to you. I have a feeling the two of us are really going to get along. I'll tell you why: because I write stories and I've heard that you are a brilliant storyteller. You tell stories to the other children, that's what their parents are saying. You tell your own Badger stories. Which I think is rather wonderful.

Louie   Let me see my subjects.

Sali   I thought we could have a go at telling a story together.

Louie   Let me see my subjects.

Sali   I'll say a bit, then you say a bit. I think you'll be really good at this.

Louie   Let me see my subjects.

Sali   One day, a little girl was walking through Willowy Wold when . . .

Louie   A bus came along and runned her over.

Sali   There aren't buses in Willowy Wold! Anyway, luckily, the girl fell just between the wheels of the bus and so she jumped right back up and went on her merry way again.

Louie   But another bus killed her. I want to see my subjects.

Sali   Luckily there was a paramedic on hand who declared that the gitl was in fact alive. So the girl skipped across the road to see her friend Badger Do Best. Your turn.

Louie   Then can I go?

Sali   Nope.

Louie   But I need to see my –

Sali   The rest of the class are not your subjects, Louie. I know it's fun to play games, but everyone in 4N is equal.

Louie   Not to me. Just ask them, they know. They're not equal to me. I need to see 4N.

Sali   You can't now, they're doing PE. Perhaps you'll be able to in a few days but we are going to do some work together first.

Louie   If you don't let me then everybody in 4N will throw themselves under the number eleven bus tomorrow morning.

Sali   Oh no, that won't happen. Ms Evitt and I sent an email to all the parents of 4N, including yours. Everybody is going to be keeping a keen eye on their children and stopping them from following your orders. Friends don't order each other around. And children listen to their parents. Children are their parents' little princes and princesses, so there'll be no more King Louie.

Silence.

Sali (*sings*)
> This is our school
> It's a peaceful place
> And a home to you and me
> Where we are free to learn,
> Grow and prosper happily.
>
> Each one of us is as unique
> As snowflakes that fall from the sky.
> And whatever our strengths may be,
> We'll try our best,
> Just like Badger Do Best,
> And treat each other respectfully.

Four

Monday, end of the school day. The classroom is empty except for
Grace *and* **Louie**. **Grace** *has her coat on and carries her book bag.*

Louie
> This girl was
> famous
> for doing the most
> after-school clubs
> in the world.
> The reason was:
> her mum had a heart as
> sour as a Haribo Tangfastic,
> and she didn't want the girl to
> mess up
> her neat house.
> So she said
> 'You have to get out of my hair,'
> and sent her to all the clubs.
> The mum felt happy even when
> the girl's eyes got baggy
> and she cried

about being so stressed.
The mum liked the girl
all tired out
cos it meant she wouldn't go
loopy
at home and
jump
on the furniture and all that.
Once, when the mum watched the daughter sleeping,
she thought,
'It's so nice and quiet and peaceful,
I hope eventually my daughter will
swim or ballet herself
till she sleeps
forever.'

Pause.

Grace   Is this fiction or non-fiction?

Louie
One day the girl's legs
felt like
they were going through
water
even though she
wasn't swimming
and her eyes felt all
droopy
and then they
closed
and then she
fell
asleep.

Grace   Then what?

Louie   Nothing. She was so tired she never woke up.

Grace   She died?

Five

Tuesday morning. 4N sit at their tables. All the children now have smiley flip charts on except **Aaron**.

Sali   But before we begin this exciting new experiment. Shhh. Before we enter the Bubble of Kindness, I would like to find out why – what's your name, little chap?

Tamaya   His name's Aaron.

Sali   Why Aaron has his frowny face on.

Lily Smith   He got the lowest mark in numeracy.

Sali   Ah. I see. Well, it's not nice to feel like you're struggling, is it? Who can tell me something that Aaron is *good* at?

Long pause.

Tamaya   Handwriting?

Sali   Are you, Aaron? Are you good at handwriting?

Aaron *shrugs.*

Esther   He is. Definitely.

Sali   So then, even though you got a lot of your sums wrong, your work would have looked really beautiful. Is that right?

Aaron *shrugs.*

Sali   It sounds to me as if that's something to feel really proud of. I think Aaron should be really happy about having such lovely handwriting. Who agrees? Put your hand up if you agree!

Most of the class put up their hands.

Sali   Who thinks that Aaron should be happy about writing beautifully?

The rest of the class raise their hands. Only **Aaron** *doesn't.*

Sali   Aaron?

Aaron *slowly puts up his hand.*

Sali   Wonderful! Now everybody's happy.

Sali *changes* **Aaron***'s flip chart to the happy face.*

Sali   Fantastic. So who would like to be first into the bubble?

All hands shoot up.

Mrs Bradley (*shouts, off*)   Wet play!

Six

Tuesday lunchtime. Wet-play chaos.

Mrs Bradley *tidies up board games, stray stationery etc.*

Sali *watches from the side, with a cup of tea and a notebook.*

A loud scream.

Mrs Bradley   Don't say the mice are back.

Tamaya *pulls a squashed and falling-to-pieces Badger out of a cupboard.*

Aaron   Badger?

Tamaya   Just shoved in there, all in pieces. Poor Badger.

Mrs Bradley   Don't look too good, do it. We'll have to order another one. Chuck that one in the bin.

Aaron   Are you sure?

Grace   He's just a toy, Aaron. He's nothing.

Reluctantly, **Tamaya** *places Badger in the bin.*

Seven

Tuesday afternoon. **Freddie** *and* **Louie** *alone in the classroom.*
Freddie *is in his PE kit and wears the latest very expensive trainers.*
He has a cut on his knee and guzzles water from a bottle.

Louie
   This boy thought his dad must love him
   so much,
   because whatever
   the boy asked for, his dad said
   yes.
   One day the boy asked if he could go out
   at night
   and ride his bike with
   no lights
   and his dad said
   yes.
   The boy hoped that his friends would be out
   but they were all kept indoors because of
   danger.
   He wondered,
   'Why doesn't my dad try to keep me indoors?'
   And
   'Why does he let me have sweets that rot my teeth?'
   And
   'Why does he do all my maths homework for me when
      I'm one of the stupidest in the class?'
   The boy thought that maybe
   his dad had swallowed a potion that meant he could
      only say
   yes.
   For a experiment, the boy asked
   if he could go and play on the
   motorway
   near his house and of course the dad said
   yes

and the boy got all run over and
died.

The end.

Freddie   Had the dad swallowed a potion?

Louie   He hadn't. The dad just didn't like speaking to his
son very much. If the dad said no to things then the boy
would be all talky and try and persuade him but if he said
yes the boy just shutted up cos he got his own way.

Eight

Later Tuesday afternoon. **Sali** *and the children of 4N sit in a circle.
The children pass a patched-together Badger around the circle. Holding
Badger means they can speak.*

Tamaya   I love Badger because he acts like a good example
to me.

Aaron   I love Badger because he tells me how to be best.

Sali   How to *do* your best. Lovely.

Lily Smith   I love Badger because he's all cuddly.

Esther   I was going to say that.

Sali   See if you can think of another reason, then.

Esther   I love Badger because he has a nice voice that
always says good things, whoever is doing his voice.

Grace   Does that even make sense? Anyway, I love
Badger except Mum says we spend too much time on him
and not enough time on learning. But I think he is kind and
he did help us learn about the Tudors.

Sali   Thank you, Grace. I wonder –

Tamaya   Freddie! Sali, Freddie's wet himself.

Freddie No.

Lily Smith He has, I can see, he has.

Sali Girls, we must remember to speak kindly to each other. Freddie, it does look as it you should change into your PE clothes, sweet one. And bring back some paper towels, please.

Freddie *exits.*

Sali Grace, I wonder why your mother thinks that about Badger and learning?

Grace Cos next year it's Year Five and she wants me to do secondary selection so my learning is really important and Mrs Bradley says it.

Sali What does Mrs Bradley say?

Grace About how we spend all our time on Badger. But Mum does like Badger too.

Sali I think you should tell your mum about how Badger helps you. About how he makes the classroom an easier place to learn in. In fact. Oh my goodness! How exciting, I've just had the most fantastic idea. Seeing as you are such a creative class and so imaginative, you should have a go at writing your very own Badger Do Best stories. They could be all about how Badger makes things easier for you. You could take them home and read them to your mums and dads.

Lily Smith Could they be as long as chapter books?

Sali Of course. And luckily for you, there is a professional author in school to give you advice. Any ideas who that might be?

Tamaya You?

Sali   Yes indeed, me. Now, I got a bit carried away with that sudden inspiration for another fun activity, where were we? Jake. 'I love Badger because . . . '

Jake   I love Badger because he has good eyes?

Nine

Tuesday, after school.

Sali   Thank you so much, I promise this won't take long.

Mrs Bradley   'S alright.

Sali   It's really not. It's against everything I believe in, asking a member of staff to stay late. It really does go beyond the call of duty, Mrs Bradley, and that hasn't gone unnoticed.

Mrs Bradley   I don't mind.

Sali   Mrs Bradley, I think you have a really special relationship with the children. I absolutely mean that – you show them such kindness and are obviously committed to their learning. It's clear you inspire them, you light up their school day in a way not many people can.

Mrs Bradley   I've always had a way with kids, dunno why.

Sali   It's a gift, isn't it?

Mrs Bradley   They like me, I like them.

Sali   I think support staff are able to have a connection with the children that is impossible for teachers.

Mrs Bradley   Well, we're not trying to teach them lessons all the time, are we? We can say how it is, and they like a bit of honesty and bluntness. I tell those Year Sixes that reckon they're mini-gangsters, you're not some big man, so why're you strutting about like that?

Sali   Ha.

Mrs Bradley   That's why teaching assistants are vital.

Sali   Well, I really am impressed.

Mrs Bradley   Thank you, Miss.

Sali   Sali, please. Which is why I thought you might be the best person to take a sneak-peak at the first draft of the Badger Do Best introductory pack. It's the resource we eventually hope to send out nationwide, and it basically sets out the principles of the system

Mrs Bradley   Right.

Sali   And how adults should interact with children.

Mrs Bradley   Lydia – Ms Newsome – did a talk on it after she came back from your course. Do you need me to make notes on it or what, Miss?

Sali   No, not so much that. I really just want to make sure we're all on the same page. I want you to be in our gang, if you like.

Pause.

Mrs Bradley   I reckon Lydia misunderstood, though. Cos she seemed to think it's all about listening to the kids, giving them their say, talking about their feelings all the time

Sali   It is. It's about giving the children a voice. The teacher guides the children towards effective communication.

Mrs Bradley   Seems like it's about telling them what to say, though.

Sali   The idea is to help shape what they say into something more appropriate. Read the pack, you'll see. We have the Department for Education in school on Friday

Mrs Bradley   I know, Verena wants me to help out.

Sali   Then you'll also know it's a good idea to read the pack, in case one of the assurance officers asks you about the system.

Mrs Bradley   If they ask, I'll tell them what I think.

Sali   Mrs Bradley, there is no place for the teaching assistant in my learning system, so I do understand why you are threatened by me. Rest assured, if the system gets rolled out across the whole school, I'll encourage Verena to find another supporting role for you. Perhaps as a playground monitor or recycling mentor

Mrs Bradley   Those are volunteer positions.

Sali   But let me summarise one of the points in the pack: when children display behaviour that is inappropriate or not in keeping with the Badger system, you don't encourage it. You don't join in with them. You model the behaviour they ought to be displaying. Mrs Bradley, a Badger Do Best school can only employ those who facilitate children doing their best.

Ten

Wednesday morning. **Louie** *and* **Jake** *are alone.* **Louie** *sits in the stock cupboard, elevated by a pile of books.* **Jake** *stands, holding an exercise book.*

Louie
     There was this boy –

Jake *puts his hands over his ears.*

Louie
     – whose parents loved to
     take photos and
     make films of him.
     They took them on sports day and

his birthday and
on every normal day, too.
All the photos went on his mum and dad's
Instagram or Facebook or
were made into those
piccybook albums online.
The boy's mum and dad loved to take pictures of him
because he was
average
and
satisfactory,
but with the photos they could turn him
perfect.
They could make his eyes bright blue
and do crops so it looked like he
won the hundred metres.
His mum and dad didn't exactly
hate him
but they just loved him more
in photos.
They took so many pictures that his eyes went
spotty
and he felt
dizzy
and he ended up getting
blind
by all the flashes and
deaf
by all the clicks. And then
he died.

Jake   I don't believe you.

Eleven

Later Wednesday morning. **Sali** *and* **Louie** *are alone.*

Sali   The idea is, each teacher has one of these sticker charts – I'm sure you'll be able to make much better ones than me because I've seen your wonderful artwork – each teacher has one of these and they carry it around with them. Now, every time you have an interaction with them, every time you speak to them, if it was a positive experience that made you feel good about yourself, I want you to give that teacher a sticker, and they can put it on their chart –

Louie   What if it's a bad experience?

Sali   – and the teacher with the most stickers on their chart at the end of the week can win a certificate or maybe a medal or a badge.

Louie   What if it's a bad experience?

Sali   We want to focus on the good experiences, so if a teacher speaks to you in a way you don't like, just don't give them a sticker. And it's only teachers, not support staff. The plan is, I'll use the sticker charts and certificate or badge or whatever you design to send out to all the schools around the country when they start doing Badger Do Best. You'll be a published designer!

Louie   When will Badger go into all the schools?

Sali   I don't know. It depends what the Department for Education say.

Louie   Who?

Sali   Some very important people from the government who are visiting school *this Friday*. Gosh!

Louie   Why do they even care about Badger?

Sali   Because children become adults, don't they? And they want children to learn the special lessons Badger teaches so they remember how to do their best when they grow up.

Louie Are they more important than you, because they decide about Badger Do Best?

Sali They might decide Badger's future but I invented him!

Louie But they decide about him.

Pause.

Sali Yes.

Louie After they decide, will you get retired?

Sali Oh no, good lord, I'm not quite there yet thank you. No, there will be lots more tasks for poor old Sali. Good thing she loves her job. Once Badger Do Best is up and running in schools, I'll start looking at how it could be used with other groups. So let's get going! I've got coloured card, double-sided sticky

Louie What groups?

Sali Choose a colour.

Louie *takes a piece of card*

Louie What other groups will use Badger?

Sali Well, occasionally adults need help to do their best too, don't they? Sometimes people get cross when things don't turn out the way they'd wanted, especially if they are a little bit broken. That's why it's good to learn how to deal with life's challenges properly at school.

Louie Broken like smashed in pieces?

Sali Broken like maybe they don't come from a loving, supportive family like yours, or they live chaotic lives and make bad decisions

Louie What's chaotic lives?

Sali   And Badger Do Best might be a way of tackling this. In the same way he helps you to be kind and have good grammar and spellings, he could help adults be independent and show them how to spend their money on the right things like fruit and vegetables. Oh yes, there's a lot of work to be done, but we can't do any of it until we've got 4N back to its old self.

Louie   So 4N are very important.

Sali   Of course!

Louie   I love 4N.

Sali (*thrilled*)   That's wonderful, Louie. Do you know, I think you might be ready to go back to 4N.

Pause.

Louie   No. I want to stay here with you forever.

Twelve

Ms Evitt   'Feel we've given Castlegrave a fair chance . . . but Grace behaving unusually . . . anxious . . . not sleeping . . . Even refusing to go to ballet . . . '

Sali   I thought you said the parents are on side?

Ms Evitt   They appeared to be. 'Can only assume it is school-related given the current unsettled situation . . . violence of last Friday . . . fact that a previously well-behaved child has been removed from class . . . since email reassuring us all would be resolved quickly, no improvement . . . left wondering if our daughter will be the next to go . . . what with secondary selection beginning next year . . . no option other than to remove Grace from Castlegrave at the end of term.' That's it: they're all going to leave. This isn't the only complaint.

Sali   This is very strange. They are little darlings when I work with them. At the moment they're writing rather wonderful Badger stories.

Ms Evitt   And Louie, how is she doing with you?

Sali   Really well.

Ms Evitt   So I can return her to 4N?

Sali   Before the assurance officers visit?

Ms Evitt   Will that be a problem?

Sali   Not at all.

Ms Evitt   Good, because I have to show the parents there's nothing to fear. The supply says the children are well-behaved in class, you have Louie under control

Sali   Yes.

Ms Evitt   Yet the parents are reporting difficult behaviour. So where's the issue?

Sali   Well, it's clear the problem must be at home.

Ms Evitt   They can't all have problems at home. It only takes one to leave, believe me. This mum talks and what she does, they'll all do. I have to nip this situation in the bud. 4N are too unpredictable to risk more change. Having seen their reaction when you first turned up on Friday, I think it's best we cancel the DfE's visit.

Sali   But Verena, having the DfE here is the only way to secure the phase two money.

Ms Evitt   Frankly, Castlegrave needs these parents more than it needs an extension. Without children like Grace, we'll be in special measures before we know it.

Sali   I wouldn't be rash.

Ms Evitt   I can't take the risk. I could lose my school, my job. I'm going to have to remove Castlegrave from the Badger Do Best pilot.

Sali   Why do that when you're so close to getting everything you want?

Ms Evitt   I don't see how, right now

Sali   Look. Let's be clever about this. Let's invite the parents in for a Sharing Circle of Trust

Ms Evitt   Absolutely not. No. That will alienate them further. They only usually come in for showing assemblies.

Sali   A showing assembly, then. We'll combine it with the DfE's visit on Friday. The children can read out the Badger Do Best stories they've been working on – it really is a credit to Castlegrave how they've built those stories, the connectives and wow words they've used – then parents and assurance officers alike will see how wonderfully they have embraced the system. You really can have it all. Because I will guarantee Castlegrave to be my phase two school.

Ms Evitt   You're able to do that?

Sali   Of course. It makes sense. After all, my modifications are based on work with a child at this school. Never underestimate my power, Verena!

Ms Evitt   And Louie will be there, at the showing assembly.

Sali   Louie will be there. Oh Verena, you'll be a heroine when you've got your shiny new extension.

Thirteen

Thursday morning. **Louie** *and* **Esther** *sit among the coats on the coat rack.*

Louie
   Her mum gave her all green smoothies and
   raw food
   and sent her to a school that had a
   healthy eating certificate
   so she didn't have
   chips every day,
   and whenever the girl complained the food was
   disgusting,
   her mum said:
   'But it will help you live forever.'
   And the mum was nearly right,
   cos the girl didn't get a heart attack or cancer or obesity.
   She lived
   on
   and
   on
   till all her friends had died and her mind wanted to sleep
      but she kept
   going
   and
   going
   till she saw climate change and the world get
   so hot by the evil sun that it was just
   her and the dinosaurs.
   And then the dinosaurs died and she was
   alone again with
   no memory about her
   friends and family.
   And then she
   died.

Louie *offers* **Esther** *a chocolate bar. She takes it.*

Mrs Bradley *enters.*

Mrs Bradley   You two, out.

Esther *runs out.*

A moment between **Louie** *and* **Mrs Bradley**.

Louie *leaves.*

Mrs Bradley *goes about tidying up the classroom.*

Mrs Bradley (*singing quietly*)
    This is our school,
    It's a poo-y place,
    And a home to poo and pee . . .

Fourteen

Later Thursday morning. **Sali** *is smiling at* **Louie**.

Sali   You see how I'm smiling at you, Louie? What should you do back?

Silence.

What should you do back?

Silence.

This exercise is called 'I Smile, You Smile'. I'm smiling, so what do you think you are supposed to do?

Silence.

Oh, you think you're very clever, don't you? Very grown-up.

Silence

We know you've been upsetting the children in 4N. I know, and Ms Evitt knows, and the parents of those children are not very happy.

Louie *smiles.*

Sali   Well, seeing as you're such a clever, grown-up little girl, I will tell you a grown-up story. It's the story of your future. Tomorrow, I will call up the assurance team at the Department for Education, and say 'I'm very sorry, I tried my best but I was unable to help Louie Saunders.' And they'll ask who Louie Saunders is, because you may feel like you're famous at Castlegrave, but in the world, in reality, you're nobody. So, I'll remind the assurance officers who you are, and they'll say, 'Well her progress was our way of testing the scheme, so we'll have to cancel it.' And that will be the end of Badger Do Best, which I've spent the last five years of my life working on, put my heart and soul into and had sleepless nights over. But it's OK, I'll get over it, I'm a grown-up. And of course Castlegrave won't get the money they were expecting from the scheme and so they won't get a new hall, and the parents and governors will be unhappy and Ms Evitt will be forced to leave her job.

But this is all terribly tedious, so let's move on to the important bit: what happens to Louie Saunders. Understandably, the parents and the governors do not want Louie in their school. She makes the children behave oddly and lost them the extension, and as there's no Ms Evitt and Sali Rayner to stick up for her – because believe me we've spent hours sticking up for you – they decide to send her to a pupil referral unit. Do you know what a pupil referral unit is?

Louie   I'm not scared.

Sali   It's where children with emotional/behavioural difficulties go if they're deemed unteachable in a normal classroom situation. Now I've worked in several PRUs, and let me tell you, they are not the places to tell stories. They kill stories. They are the places children go when they've been given up on, and *that's* scary. The rest of your story writes itself. No education means no job means not very much else.

Louie   Kings don't need jobs

Sali   YOU ARE NOT A KING.

Pause.

And I don't think you should be given up on, so it will weigh heavily on my mind when they send you there. But in time, like Ms Newsome and Ms Evitt, like the parents who are so concerned about you right now, and like the children of 4N, *I will forget about you.*

Louie   It's not my fault Castlegrave won't have a extension.

Sali   Louie, if you don't want to spend the rest of your school life stuck in a PRU colouring in triangles, you could decide that you are going to cooperate. You could sit sensibly with 4N and then read out part of a Badger Do Best story tomorrow with the rest of your class. You could smile nicely and bow when everyone claps. That's what you could do to stay at Castlegrave.

Louie   Like a deal?

Sali   Like how if you tidy away your things, you get to go out to play. Yes, like a deal.

Fifteen

Thursday lunchtime. **Sali** *stands between* **Louie** *and a patched-up Badger Do Best.* **Ms Evitt** *looks on.*

Sali   And how do you feel, Louie?

Louie   Before I feel very upset and angry with Badger but now I know that only the person moving him tells him what to do. So I don't feel angry any more.

Sali   Well done for sharing how you feel. What do you think you should have done differently?

Louie   I should have done my best.

Sali   Is there anything else you'd like to say?

Louie   Sorry, Badger.

Sali   Now you can shake hands.

Louie *shakes Badger's hand.*

Sali   I am very proud of you for doing your best.

Ms Evitt   And so am I. I'm very, very proud, Louie. Would you take Badger back to the office for me now?

Louie   Yes, Ms Evitt.

She leaves.

Ms Evitt   Phew!

Sali   There goes a girl transformed by Badger Do Best. I think I'm going to cry.

Ms Evitt   Did I tell you some local papers and a photographer are coming tomorrow?

Sali   Let's just savour this victory. It's so important to congratulate oneself on these golden moments. Well done us.

Ms Evitt   Yes. It's just the journalists would like to interview you after the assembly and wondered if there's any literature we could send them through.

Sali   My PA will send them through a biog and some Badger Do Best blurb.

Ms Evitt   Great. I'll let them know.

Sali   Mrs Bradley said she's been asked to assist tomorrow. I don't think we need any extra help do we? The scheme aims to cut out the need for extra assistance in the classroom, such is the control Badger allows the teacher.

Ms Evitt   I know, but let's take no chances and have all hands on deck.

Sali   I get the feeling Mrs Bradley isn't very supportive of the system. The last thing I want is someone undermining –

Ms Evitt   She's far from progressive, I know, but the kids love her and she's reliable. I'll let those papers know you'll be sending some stuff through.

Sali   Right-o.

Sixteen

Louie *and Badger Do Best are alone.*

Louie   What would you do differently next time, Badger?

She puts her ear to Badger's mouth to hear the answer.

Seventeen

Friday morning. Class 4N. **Ms Evitt, Mrs Bradley** *and* **Sali** *are at one end of the room.*

Ms Evitt   Good morning, children, good morning, everybody.

Children   Good morning, Ms Evitt, good morning, everybody.

Ms Evitt   Thank you so much for being patient while we worked out the seating, there's a lot of us to squeeze in today. I'd like to welcome all the parents and guardians who were able to make our assembly, the representatives from the Department for Education and Mary from the (*Insert name of local paper.*) who will be taking pictures, so children try not to be put off. As many of you know, this hasn't been the easiest of terms so far, but the pupils of 4N have learned a lot and are now a more robust class, thanks to the work of

Sali Rayner who we've been lucky enough to have with us over the past week. Sali.

Sali   My goodness! What wonderful, wonderful children we have here. I know you must be so proud, parents. I'm thrilled that you are all here to listen to these wonderful stories that 4N have written about Badger Do Best, the character from my fiction books and learning system. I hope that through listening to these stories, you will come to love Badger as much as we do and that this marks the beginning of a unification of school, community and Badger Do Best. The first story, one I think is very inventive, explores Badger's arrival at Willowy Wold. OK, 4N? Remember, big voices.

Aaron (*reading*)   Once upon a time in a place called Willowy Wold peacefully lived Badger Do Best and his friends. But this story starts before Badger Do Best moved to Willowy Wold, and it was just Diggin Burrows, Lil Harvest Mouse and Tabby Miaow –

She gestures to the characters on the wall.

Lily Smith (*reading*)   Amazingly, all the animals in Willowy Wold were friends. Surprisingly, the animals never fell out. And then one day a badger called Badger Do Best – (*gestures to him on wall*) arrived. Lil Harvest Mouse saw him from the distance and she wondered who he was because she didn't know him yet.

Tamaya (*reading*)   Meanwhile, Diggin and Tabby were walking down the path towards where he was and he came towards them and smiled and said 'I'm Badger Do Best and I can help you do your best too.' The animals thought doing their best was a very intelligent idea.

Esther (*reading*)   Badger Do Best did things like the Shower of Positive Praise and the Bubble of Kindness. He told them not to worry about being bad at maths because they have nice handwriting. Badger told them they were all unique and special and then he made them do the same as him and the same as each other. He said that he'd only listen to them if they talked in the way that he liked.

Pause.

The children look directly at the audience.

Esther   He wants us to speak just like him.

Jake   Badger Do Best wants to keep us small and stop us asking questions. He tells us we're fourth set from the top when really we're second from the bottom because he doesn't want us to be dissatisfied in case it makes us unruly. He likes us nice and cosy where we are. Badger Do Best's not really real and his name shouldn't even have any capitals. But he isn't the only baddie in the story.

Grace   There is the person who made him up completely in her head. She is called Sali which is a normal name and she puts an 'i' at the end to make her interesting but nothing can make her interesting. And if you count the number of times she says 'I' when she's talking, you would get a very high number. But she isn't the only baddie in the story.

Sali   Well. I –

Mrs Bradley *stands.*

Sali   This is ridiculous.

Ms Evitt *also stands.*

Sali *sits.*

Freddie   Badger Do Best sweeps up trouble and chaos and underclass and unrest and broken things and makes them go away. They want us to learn early not to be properly heard because then we won't get rowdy when we are ignored later on. They think Badger will make people be happy about war and no jobs. But they aren't the only baddies in the story.

Louie   Because Badger Do Best has Sali's voice and Sali
has the government's voice and the government has your
voice. It only does what you let it.

You think you're best in the world cos you tell us,

'Your best is good enough. But if you're not level four by the
end of this year let's get you a statement.

Turn autistic and be a maths genius.

He's very creative. She's the sporty one. He has a science
brain.

Are you happy?

Safety first.

Bring a permission slip.

No exploring. 999, remember it.

Tell an adult.'

> You think Badger will get us quick to
> our future,
> make us what we're
> supposed to be.
> But
> we could make up stories.
> We could be
> inappropriate.
> We could have
> danger,
> and get
> ideas.
> We could be
> unhappy.
> We could
> save the day.
>
> I'm so precious I need a
> baby on board sign.

Give me my five a day or
I'll call ChildLine cos I'm worth it.

I am unique
as a snowflake.

What are you so frightened of?

The children all look into the distance as if there is something dreadful ahead of them.

Miss Jackson *enters. She belongs to the future. She wears a 'Teacher of the Week' badge.*

Miss Jackson   Once upon a time, deep, deep in a willowy wood was Willowy Wold, where Badger Do Best *(Gestures to the cuddly toy Badger on the wall.)* and his friends lived in peace and harmony. Nobody knew about those friendly creatures who shared a village in the woods. Nobody that is except . . .

Children *(whisper)*   4J.

Badger Do Best   And that was how the girl learnt she would never change the world.

The End.

For a complete listing of Bloomsbury
Methuen Drama titles, visit:

www.bloomsbury.com/drama

Follow us on Twitter and keep up to date
with our news and publications

@MethuenDrama